Wire & Beaded Wedding Jewelry

Wire & Beaded Wedding Jewelry

34 step-by-step projects
for tiaras, necklaces, hair accessories,
table decorations, and more

Linda Jones

CICO BOOKS
LONDON NEW YORK

This book is dedicated to my partner, Chris, who had to put up with my long hours of dedicated designing and writing—but I surfaced for air in the end and I thank him for his patience and love throughout!

Published in 2012 by CICO Books
An imprint of Ryland Peters & Small
519 Broadway, 5th Floor,   20–21 Jockey's Fields,
New York, NY 10012   London WC1R 4BW

www.cicobooks.com

10 9 8 7 6 5 4 3 2 1

ISBN 978-1-907563-84-3

Printed in China

Editor: Sarah Hoggett
Design: David Fordham
Photography: Geoff Dann (steps) and Stuart West (styled shots)
Stylist: Luis Peral-Aranda and Sophie Martell
Illustration: Stephen Dew

Contents

Introduction

When I set out to write and design this book, the hardest thing was deciding what to leave out–wedding jewelry, tiara designs, and headdress styles are limitless! You can be inspired by so many themes! In the end, however, I decided to base the book around the seasons of the year, as this can often dictate the shape and style of the bride's dress, as well as the overall color scheme.

Traditionally, gold, pearl, and crystal color beads are most frequently associated with weddings, but why not create accessories with a different palette, using the combined colors of the bride and groom's birthstones, or the seasonal colors of nature (my inspiration for the autumnal amber and bronze beads used in the Leafy crown on page 76)?

Once the theme has been chosen, you can develop this throughout all the wedding accessories, weaving continuity through color, shape, and style, from the initial invitation right through to the bridesmaids' jewelry, the bride's mother's hat pin, and even the table decorations at the reception.

Not only will each handcrafted wedding piece reflect your own personal taste and style to make the day really unique and especially memorable, it will also be key to cutting down your costs.

Once you've decided on what you want to make, adapt the projects to suit your style and theme, and don't be afraid to mix and match different pieces together from the various chapters. Provided you keep to matching color schemes, it will all look unified on the day. Also, don't feel you have to make everything yourself; you will be surprised by how much family members and friends will want to help to make the day extra special and therefore be very willing to get together at evening or weekends to help create the invitations and table decorations.

Designing wedding jewelry

Making jewelry for such a special day can be quite a daunting prospect, so let me give you an insight into some of the factors that I consider before I embark on a bridal jewelry commission. First, I ask to see a sketch or photo of the bride's dress, or even the dress itself, to get an idea of the shape, style, and color. If the dress has a lot of beading or embroidered detail, I can use this as inspiration for the tiara design, echoing both the style and motifs; also, any color or beading on the dress can be matched up with similar beads within the bride's jewelry. If, on the other hand, the gown is very plain in style, a simple headdress, rather than a fussy, over-decorated one, will be far more in keeping. The shape and cut of the outfit also help determine the design of extra accessories and jewelry such as a necklace, bracelet, or earrings. For instance, a plunge or rounded neckline will provide inspiration for the necklace style and shape, while a sleeveless dress will give you scope for an inventive bracelet design. And a sample of the dress fabric is often useful in helping you select ivory or cream pearl beads of exactly the right tone.

Second, I ask the bride how she is considering wearing her hair, as this can dictate the style of tiara design. For instance, if she is going to wear her hair up, this will help anchor any hair accessories or tiara into a structured style. If she has short, fine, or loose hair, however, it might be better to recommend a hairband-style tiara, which will support itself. Also, don't forget to make a note of the bride's hair color, so that you can match hairpins to secure the tiara band in place, making them as invisible as possible.

Third, take a good objective look at the bride's face shape, as this will help you to design a tiara that complements her face. A tiara that tapers on each side or one with some central height, for instance, is far more flattering to a round face, while a lower headband, worn toward the back of the head, suits longer faces and will not accentuate them.

Fourth, remember to ask the bride if she is going to be wearing a veil. This will help you to decide on the size of tiara to make, as it will need to be positioned in front of the veil comb. You could also design the comb decoration at the back of the head to match and blend with the tiara at the front. If, however, she is not wearing a veil, you could ask if she is interested in some decorative accessory for the back of her hair, such as hairpins with beaded ornamentation.

Finally, ask if there is a theme for the special day. For instance, if the reception is being held in a historic building, the bride might want to choose that period in history as a style. Alternatively, there may be a particular color theme for the wedding: ask about the color of the bridesmaids' dresses or the flowers in the bride's bouquet, as this can be reiterated in any beaded items such as necklaces and bracelets. A motif that is significant to both bride and groom can also trigger a theme. All these little insights can be used as inspiration to create pieces of jewelry that are completely unique and very personal.

Tools

One of the joys of making wire and beaded jewelry is that you require very little in the way of specialty tools and equipment– and everything you need is readily available from craft suppliers, mail-order catalogs, and, of course, the Internet at very affordable prices. Here are my suggestions for a basic tool kit.

Hammer and flat steel stake

These tools are used to flatten and toughen wire motifs (see page 15). Specialty jewelry hammers are generally smaller and lighter than general-purpose household hammers, but you can use any hammer as long as one end has a flat, smooth, polished surface. Steel stakes can be bought from specialty jewelry stores, but any flat steel surface will do, provided the top surface has no bumps or abrasions–otherwise the wire will pick up any irregularities that are present.

Ring mandrel, or triblet

Available from specialty jewelry stores, a mandrel is used to form circular shapes such as rings and bangles. Alternatively, shape your wire around any cylindrical object of the appropriate size.

Wire cutters

Several kinds of wire cutter are available, but I find that "side cutters" are the most useful, as they have small, tapered blades that can cut into small spaces. Remember to hold the cutters perpendicular to the wire when cutting to achieve a clean, flush cut.

Pliers

From top to bottom: Round-, flat-, and chain-nose pliers. Round-nose pliers have round, tapered shafts; they are used to coil and bend wire into small loops and curves and to make jump rings. Chain-nose and flat-nose pliers are both used to grip the wire firmly as you work and to bend it at right angles and angular shapes. However, chain-nose pliers are tapered and narrow and, therefore, extremely useful when working on intricate, more delicate pieces. They are also essential for neatening ends.

Jig and pegs

A jig consists of a base board with evenly spaced holes and movable pegs with tops of different diameters, which you arrange in a pattern. You then wrap wire around the pegs to create a wire design. Some jig grids are based on a square, and some on the diagonal, so you may have to alter the project patterns slightly to suit your make of jig.

Hand drill and vise

These are not essential tools, but they are useful for twisting several lengths of wire together (see page 19). A small vise that you can attach to the edge of your work table is also a helpful tool to have if you are braiding wire, as it holds one end of the wires firmly together while you work—although you could ask a friend to help.

Wire

Wire is available in many thicknesses, types, and colors and can be manipulated into all kinds of shapes. Colored, copper, and plated wires can be bought from most craft and hobby stores, as well as from bead suppliers. With the exception of precious-metal wire, wire is generally sold in spools of a pre-measured length. Precious-metal wire is bought by length, the price being calculated by weight.

Colored wires are usually copper based, with enamel coatings, which means that you must not hammer or over-manipulate them, as this might damage or even remove the surface color.

Instead of precious-metal wires, I almost always use gold- or silver-plated wires, which are far less expensive and will not tarnish so quickly. If you do use precious-metal wires, always store them in self-seal bags to prevent them from tarnishing.

Which wire to use

26-gauge (0.4-mm)	Use for binding, knitting, and weaving
24-gauge (0.6-mm)	Use for threading small, delicate beads, and for binding and twisting
20-gauge (0.8-mm)	Use for general-purpose jewelry work
18-gauge (1-mm)	Use for chunkier pieces and ring shanks
14-gauge (1.5-mm)	Use for bold statement jewelry
12-gauge (2-mm)	Use for very chunky jewelry, bangles, and tiara bases

Wire thicknesses

All these kinds of wire come in different thicknesses or "gauges." Depending on where you buy your wire, different measurements are used to denote the thickness. The chart above will enable you to convert quickly from one system to another and to ascertain what thickness is best for your purpose. The lower the gauge number, the thicker the wire—so 18-gauge wire is thicker than 26-gauge wire.

Wire is available in almost every color of the rainbow!

Beads

From traditional pearls and semi-precious stones to sparkling iridescent crystals and metallics with an edgier, more contemporary feel, there are so many beads to choose from that you're guaranteed to find something to make your wedding jewelry really special. The range of colors is equally vast: white and ivory-colored pearls to match the wedding gown; pretty pastel hues; sizzling hot shades of orange, pink, azure blue, and lime. No matter how exotic and unusual your color scheme is, you'll find beads to suit it!

Metallic

If you wish to understate the color in your wedding and create a more contemporary feel to the jewelry, gold and silver beads work beautifully together. You can source precious-metal beads or, if your budget is tight, choose from a wide range of plastic, metal-coated beads.

Faceted crystals

These beads come in every color of the rainbow and can be acrylic or glass and shaped and faceted in a variety of styles and sizes. Their colors are particularly vibrant and will infuse a tiara, necklace, bracelet, or earrings with instant sparkle and radiance. Swarovski crystals are probably the most famous brand in this category, but for a less expensive option, use Czech glass crystal.

Semi-precious stones

Natural semi-precious stones add instant beauty and richness to wedding jewelry and can be included for symbolic reasons: using the bride's birthstone or combining the bride and groom's birthstone into the wedding color theme. The organic, uneven shapes and cuts of stones blend well with pearls and crystals.

Seed beads

Seed beads are very small, round, glass beads, ranging from under a millimeter to several millimeters in diameter. They are available in most colors, as well as transparent and silver-lined, and add delicacy to your tiara decorations. The most popular sizes are between 9/0 (15 beads per inch/2.5 cm) and 11/0 (20 beads per inch/2.5 cm); the larger the size number, the smaller the bead!

Pearls

Pearls are probably the most traditional beads for weddings, especially in white, cream, and ivory colors, but you will now find ranges of every color combination—soft peaches and dusty pinks, as well as vibrant, bold tones. Glass pearls have a stunning opalescent sheen, but if your budget is tight, you can source less expensive acrylic ones. Look after your pearls, as they can scratch easily, and avoid spraying hairspray or perfume near to them, as this can dull the finish.

Basic techniques

Threading beads and making a link

The basic principle is to construct a neat circle of wire (known as a "link") at each
end of the bead, which is then used to suspend the bead from a chain or to connect
one bead to another.

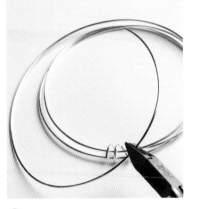

1 Working from the spool, thread your chosen bead onto the wire, leaving about ½ in. (1 cm) of wire extending on each side.

2 Remove the bead and cut the wire with your wire cutters.

3 Thread the bead back onto the cut wire. Holding the wire vertically, with the bead in the center, use the tips of your round-nose pliers to bend the wire at a right angle, at the point where it touches the bead.

4 Hold and squeeze the very end of the bent wire tightly with your round-nose pliers and curl it around to form a small circle, following the contour of your pliers. It is better to do this in several short movements, repositioning the pliers as necessary, than to attempt to make one continuous circle. Repeat steps 2–4 to form another link at the other end of the bead.

5 When you've threaded the bead, hold each link firmly in the jaws of your pliers and twist until both links face the same way, otherwise they will twist around when linked together as a chain.

Neatening ends

When you've wrapped one piece of wire around another–when making a clasp, for example–it's important to neaten the ends to prevent any sharp pieces from sticking out.

Snip the wire as close as possible to the stem, and then press it firmly with your flat- or chain-nose pliers to flatten it against the piece of jewelry. For an extra-smooth finish, you can use a small needle file or sandpaper to file away any roughness.

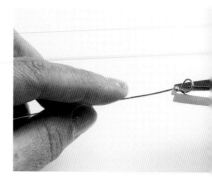

Making a head pin

If you want to suspend a bead from a chain, you need only a suspension link at one end of the bead. At the other end, you need to make what is known as a "head pin," which is virtually invisible but prevents the bead from slipping off the wire.

Above are some examples of handmade head pins. Top row, from left to right: standard, closed spiral, flattened spiral; bottom row, from left to right: hammered end, "Greek key," triangle.

1 Working from the spool, thread your chosen bead onto the wire and let it slip down, leaving the end exposed.

2 Using the tips of your round-nose pliers, make a tiny curl at one end of the wire. Squeeze this curl flat with your flat-nose pliers to create a knob of doubled wire.

3 Push your bead right up to the "head pin" and snip the wire, leaving a stem about ½ in. (1 cm) long. Form a link at this end of the wire, using your round-nose pliers. If the hole in the bead is large and it slips over the head pin, bend the head pin at a right angle, so that the bead sits on top of it like a tiny shelf. (Alternatively, slide a small seed bead onto the wire first to act as a stopper.)

The head pin (on the right-hand end of the bead) is unobtrusive, but it prevents the bead from slipping off the wire.

Making spirals

There are two kinds of spiral: open and closed. Each is formed in the same way, the only difference being whether or not any space is left between the coils. Both types of spiral begin by curling a circle at the end of the wire. If you want to make a closed spiral without a center hole, make a head pin first and curl the remaining wire around the doubled-up end.

An open spiral has evenly spaced gaps between the coils. A closed spiral is made in the same way, but with no spaces in between the coils.

1 Begin by curling a small circle at the end of the wire, using the tips of your round-nose pliers. Make this circle as round as possible, as the rest of the spiral will be shaped around it.

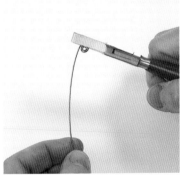

2 Grip the circle tightly in the jaws of your flat-nose pliers and begin curling the wire around it. For a closed spiral, shown here, butt each coil up tightly against the previous one. For an open spiral, leave space between one coil and the next, making sure that the spaces are even.

3 When the spiral is the size you want, leave about ½ in. (1 cm) of wire to form a suspension link, curling the projecting end of wire into a small loop in the opposite direction to the spiral.

Work hardening

Work hardening means toughening the wire. One method is to hammer the piece on a clean, smooth, dent-free steel stake (see page 10). With colored wire, use a nylon hammer or place a cloth over the piece before you hammer, as the colored coating can rub off. This technique is not suitable for small jump rings or links, as it will distort their shape; see page 18 for how to work harden jump rings.

Place your piece on the stake and "stroke" hammer it, bringing the flat part of the hammer down at 90° to the piece. Hammer your piece standing up, so that the hammer head hits the wire squarely, rather than at an angle, which could create texturing in the metal. After several strokes, you will see the wire flattening, spreading, and work hardening.

Spiral S-link

This timeless chain-linking system is simple and stylish and will turn any suspended bead necklace into a decorative masterpiece.

Here, spiral S-links have been connected together into a chain, using a pair of jump rings (see page 17) between each two units to add extra security. If you want to add color to the chain, thread a bead onto your cut wire in Step 1 and create the spiral S-shape around it.

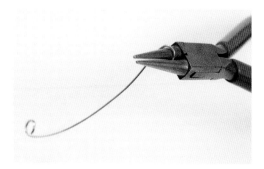

The completed spiral S-link.

1 Cut 4 in. (10 cm) of 20-gauge (0.8-mm) wire. Curl a large circle at each end, around the widest part of the shaft of your round-nose pliers. The circles should curl in opposite directions.

2 Using your flat-nose pliers, curl each end of the wire inward in a tight spiral until they meet in the center.

Using a jig

Before you try a jig project, place your pegs in your chosen design and then wrap a piece of cord or string approximately the same gauge as the wire that will be used around the pegs, following the pattern. Measure the amount of cord or string that you have used so that you know how much wire you will need to make the project, and then cut your wire to this length. To work harden your jig unit, flatten it in your flat-nose pliers or gently "stroke" hammer (see page 15) the outer extremities of the motif.

1 Following your chosen pattern, place the pegs in the jig. Using your round-nose pliers, form a link at one end of your length of wire and slip it over the first peg, securing it in place.

2 Pull the wire around the pegs, following the pattern. You will need to keep pushing the wire down to the base of the pegs in order to keep the motif reasonably flat. Carefully remove the wire unit from the pegs so that it doesn't spring out of shape. If you have wire left over when you've made the unit, simply snip it off.

Making jump rings

Jump rings are used to connect units together. You can buy them ready-made, but it is well worth learning how to make them yourself, as you can then match the jump rings to the color and size of wire that you are using. It is also much less expensive to make them yourself!

Jump rings are made by forming a wire coil around the shaft of your round-nose pliers, out of which you snip individual rings as required. When you bring the wire around the pliers to begin forming the second ring of the coil, it needs to go below the first coil, nearer your hand. This keeps the wire on the same part of the pliers every time. If you bring the wire around and above the first ring of the coil, the jump rings will taper, following the shape of the pliers' shaft. You can also make jump rings by wrapping wire around a cylindrical object, such as a knitting needle, large nail, or the barrel of a pen, depending on the diameter required.

Jump rings can also be linked together to create a chain. From top to bottom: silver jump rings linked together; copper jump rings interspersed with pairs of smaller silver jump rings; copper jump rings.

1 Working from the spool, wrap the wire five or six times around one shaft of your round-nose pliers, curling it around the same part of the pliers every time to create an even coil.

2 Remove the coil from the pliers and cut if off from the spool of wire using your wire cutters.

3 Find the cut end and, using your wire cutters, snip upward into the next ring of the coil above, thereby cutting off a full circle. Continue cutting each ring off the coil in turn to obtain more jump rings.

Using jump rings to connect units

Jump rings are used to connect units together; they can also be joined together to make a decorative chain.

To toughen (or work harden) the jump rings, carefully move the two ends of the ring just past one another, holding one side with your flat-nose pliers and the other side with your chain-nose pliers; this manipulation will provide tension, enabling the cut ends to sit more securely together. Spend a little extra time checking that there are no gaps between your links, so that when you come to wear the piece, you know it won't all fall apart. For extra security and peace of mind, link units together with two or three jump rings instead of just one.

Using your flat-nose pliers, open one of the jump rings sideways (like a door), so that you do not distort the shape. Loop the open jump ring through the links of the beads or individual chain units and close it with flat-nose pliers.

Fish-hook clasp

The most commonly used clasp is the fish-hook, which is also one of the simplest to create.

This hook-shaped clasp is both decorative and functional.

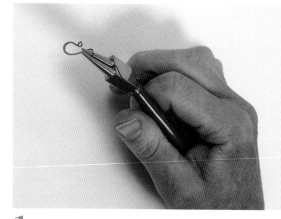

1 Working directly from a spool of wire, curl the end of the wire into a small loop, using the tips of your round-nose pliers. Reposition your pliers on the other side of the wire, just under the loop, and curl the wire in the opposite direction around the wider part of the pliers to form the fish-hook clasp.

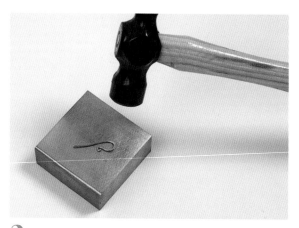

2 Cut the wire off the spool, leaving about ½ in. (1 cm) to form a link (see page 13). If you wish, you can gently hammer the hook on a steel stake to work harden and flatten it slightly, thereby making it stronger and more durable.

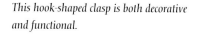

The "eye" of the fastener

This "eye" can be used to complete all clasps.

The "eye" can be linked to the ends of a necklace or bracelet directly or via jump rings.

1 Working from the spool, curl a piece of wire around the widest part of your round-nose pliers about 1 in. (2.5 cm) from the end of the wire to form a loop, crossing the end of the wire over itself.

2 Wrap the extending wire around the stem, just under the loop, to secure.

3 Cut the wire off the spool, leaving ½ in. (1 cm) extending. Squeeze the cut end flat against the stem, making sure no spiky ends protrude. Using round-nose pliers, form a link with the extending wire (see page 13).

4 Gently hammer the "eye" on a steel stake to flatten and toughen it. Do not hammer the wires that have been wrapped over the stem or you will weaken them.

Twisting wires together

Twisting wires together is not only fun and quick, but can provide a bolder, more metallic feel to your pieces. I recommend using a vise and hand drill for this technique, as it is both fast and effective. If you do not have these tools, however, attach one end of your wires to a door handle or nail and the other to a wooden handle, such as a wooden spoon and, keeping the wires straight and taut, twist them in the same direction until you achieve the effect you want.

Always twist wires of the same thickness. If you end up with an uneven twist or bumps in your wire, some of the wires were longer or looser than others! Bind the ends of the wires with masking tape. Place one end in the chuck of the hand drill and the other end in the vise. Hold the hand drill so that the wires are straight and taut, and gently turn the handle in one direction. (Do not twist too much or the wires will lose flexibility and become weak and brittle.) When the twist is complete, remove the wires from the hand drill and vise and snip off the taped ends.

Tiara bases

Tiara bases and manufactured headbands are all readily available from bead suppliers, but in my opinion, they are not very flexible and are often too big and slightly uncomfortable, especially as heads come in all shapes and sizes. It is easy to make your own base from wire and below are some suggestions. To work out how much wire you need, use a piece of string or cord as a measure. Most bases are between 10 and 12 in. (25 and 30 cm).

Once the base is complete, you can wire decorative stems to the front and sides. The tiara can be secured on the head by threading hair grips through the links at each end of the base.

Plain wire base

This is so simple, it barely needs any explanation!

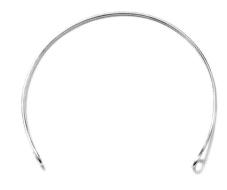

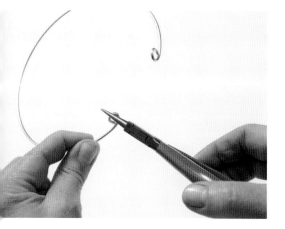

1 Using heavy-duty wire cutters, cut a piece of 12-gauge (2-mm) wire about 1 in. (2.5 cm) longer than required. Curve the wire into a crescent shape by wrapping it around a cylindrical object such as a bottle or jar. Using your round-nose pliers, make a link (see page 13) at each end. You're now ready to wire on your decorations!

Beaded base

A beaded base looks very pretty in its own right and barely requires any other form of embellishment.

1 Cut your tiara base from 20-gauge (0.8-mm) wire and shape it into a crescent. Using your round-nose pliers, curl a link at one end only. Thread the other end with a selection of pearl or crystal beads (or colored beads, to match the theme of your wedding). Use your round-nose pliers to make a link at the other end. Remember to leave a small space between the beads and the end link, as you will need to allow space for the tiara stems to be secured in place.

Twisted base

This is another decorative base that can either be used as it is or embellished with decorative stems.

1 Cut three or four lengths of 20-gauge (0.8-mm) wire 12–14 in. (30–35 cm) long, and tape the ends together with a sliver of masking tape. Place one end in the chuck of a hand drill and the other end in a table vise, securing both very tightly. Twist the handle of the drill to create your twisted cable. Using heavy-duty wire cutters, cut off the taped ends.

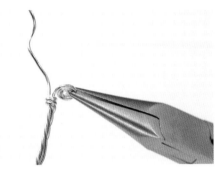

2 Unravel the twisted ends to reveal about 1½ in. (4 cm) of wire. Wrap one of the wires around all of the projecting stems, cut off any excess, and neaten the end. Repeat this with all the wires, apart from the last two. Form a small, closed spiral (see page 15) with the second-to-last wire and flatten this over the wrapped stem.

3 Using your round-nose pliers, make a wrapped link (see page 18) with the last projecting wire. Hammer the end of the loop to flatten and work harden it (see page 15). Repeat steps 2 and 3 at the other end of the twisted cable.

Tips for top tiaras!

- Always make the stems of tiara decorations at least 1 in. (2.5 cm) longer than you want the finished height to be, so that you have enough wire to wrap around the tiara base to fix the decoration in place.
- If you have excess wire on a stem, don't rush to cut it off: instead, use it to make a small, closed spiral (see page 15) that can be flattened onto the piece and used as extra decoration. (You'll need about 1 in./2.5 cm extra to be able to do this.)
- When wiring tiara decorations to a base, use an odd number of stems (three, five, or seven), so that you have a proportional balance.
- Always start wiring your tiara decorations from the center of the base, working alternately on each side, as this will help you keep the design symmetrical.

- If your tiara stems feel a little wobbly after you have attached them to the base, wrap fine wire, wire with beads, or even ribbon around the base and stems to provide extra security.
- It is easier to work with short lengths of wire, as longer ones can accumulate kinks along the way; 12 in. (30 cm) is long enough to manipulate when twisting and binding. If you run out, add a new piece of wire by wrapping and securing it over the point where you left off.
- If you're making twisted stems or twisting wires to form a base, remember that the twisting process will shorten the overall length of the piece, so allow a little more wire than usual; you can always cut off any excess.

Decorative tiara stems

There are numerous tiara stems, branches, or twigs that can be created out of wire and beads and I'm sure that, with a little practice, you'll soon be inventing your own unique shapes and styles!

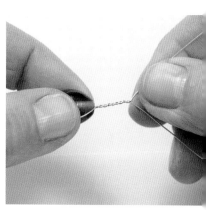

Beaded twist

This is one of the simplest decorative stems to make.

1 Begin by cutting a length of 26-gauge (0.4-mm) wire about two and a half times longer than you want the finished piece to be. Thread this wire with a bead, sliding it to the center of the length. Bring the wires around the bead and cross them over where they intersect.

2 Hold the bead tightly in your fingers and twist the wires together, keeping them in a V-shape, to gain an even, twisted stem. Cut off any uneven wires at the end.

Flower stem

In this variation on the beaded twist, small beads encircle one large bead to create a daisy-type flower.

1 Cut a length of 26-gauge (0.4-mm) wire and thread it with small "petal" seed beads. Push the beads to the center of the length and bring the ends together to check that you have enough to fit snugly around the perimeter of your central bead.

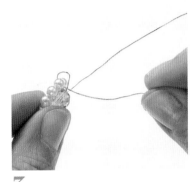

2 Twist the wires where they cross for a couple of turns and straighten out the projecting ends. Thread both these wires through the hole of the central bead and over the twist.

3 Push the central bead into the middle of the beaded loop. Take one of the projecting wires and loop it around the beaded frame, pulling it tight to secure.

4 Hold the flower in one hand and the projecting stems in a V-shape in the other. Twist the flower to obtain an even, twisted stem. Cut off any uneven ends.

Beaded twist variations

Using the same methods, you can create many variations on the basic twisted stem. Here are a few samples of different groups of beads to inspire you.

For a different take on the beaded twist, try adding different numbers and sizes of beads to the stem.

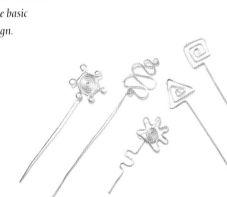

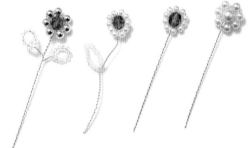

Beaded "leaves" made from tiny seed beads add an extra dimension to the basic flower stem design.

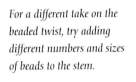

For something a little more elaborate, why not form individual "petals" or heart shapes on your twisted stems?

Omit beads altogether and form wire into spiraled shapes (see page 15) or "wiggles."

Chapter 1

SPRING

Spring leaves card
Bud and leaf tiara
Leaf and flower necklace
Lily headband
Birthstone bracelet
Pearly swirl bracelet
Bouquet brooch
Table flowers

With buds about to burst into bloom, spring is such a lovely time to "tie the knot"! The leaf- and flower-inspired designs in this chapter capture the essence of new growth in nature and symbolize the bride and groom's blossoming love. The color theme is green and cream.

Spring leaves card

This invitation card has as its centerpiece a bouquet of fresh spring leaves, in celebration of new growth and the beginning of the bride and groom's life together. The design can be made without the beads, making it more practical to send through the mail.

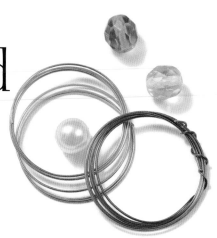

1 Working from a spool of 20-gauge (0.8-mm) wire, thread a 6-mm bead onto the spool and, using your round-nose pliers, curl the very end of the wire into a half-circle. Push the bead into the curve of the wire and wrap the wire tightly around the perimeter of the bead to enclose it completely. Using your flat-nose pliers, carefully curl the wire around the bead several times to make an open spiral (see page 15) about ½ in. (1 cm) in diameter.

2 Place the tips of your round-nose pliers about ½ in. (1 cm) from the spiraled bead and bend the wire at 90° and then back in the opposite direction. Holding the working wire firmly in your flat-nose pliers, bring it down around the side of the bead until it is opposite the tip of the unit. Straighten out the stem and cut the wire from the spool, leaving about 2 in. (5 cm) projecting.

You will need
(for each card)

20-gauge (0.8-mm) silver-plated wire
25-gauge (0.5-mm) green wire
2 x 6-mm green beads
1 x 6-mm pearl bead
3 x 4-in. (8 x 10-cm) piece of backing card
6 x 4-in. (148 x 105-mm/A6) card blank
Masking tape
Double-sided tape
Wire cutters
Round-, flat-, and chain-nose pliers
Hammer and steel stake
Scissors
Safety pin

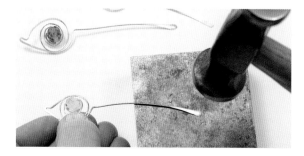

3 Carefully hammer the edges and ends of the spiral unit, taking care not to smash the bead. Repeat steps 1–3 to make two more "leaf" units.

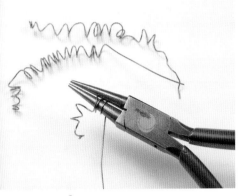

4 Working directly from a spool of 25-gauge (0.5-mm) green wire, curl the wire around the shaft of your round-nose pliers (or around a knitting needle) in a random fashion to make a tendril about 2 in. (5 cm) long, with a 2-in. (5-cm) straight stem. Repeat to make two more of these tendrils.

5 Place the "leaf" units and tendrils together in a bunch and bind the stems together with a sliver of masking tape. Working from a spool of 20-gauge (0.8-mm) wire, make a coil large enough to slip over the taped area of your stems, as when making jump rings (see page 17). Slide the coil over all the stems and squeeze the top and bottom rings with your chain-nose pliers to secure it around the wires.

6 Using a safety pin, pierce a hole in the backing card. Push the ends of the green tendrils through the hole and secure on the back with double-sided tape. Stick the backing card to your card blank with doubled-sided tape.

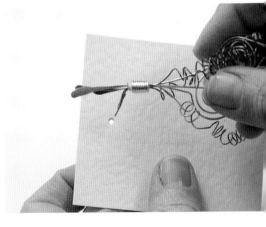

Bud and leaf tiara

A stylish tiara such as this, with its pearl "flower buds" and sparkling silver "leaves," is guaranteed to make any bride feel like a princess on her special day. Although this design looks complex, it is actually quite simple to make. I hope it will spark off ideas for a headpiece using beads of your choice to go with the bride's dress or the overall color scheme of the wedding. Freshwater pearls and crystal beads, or ivory and salmon pearls, make stunning combinations.

You will need

24-, 20-, and 12-gauge (0.6-mm, 0.8-mm, and 2-mm) silver-plated wire

Approx. 8 x 14-mm, 7 x 8-mm, and 18 x 6-mm ivory pearl beads

Round silver ribbon

Double-sided tape

Wire cutters

Round-, flat-, and chain-nose pliers

Hammer and steel stake

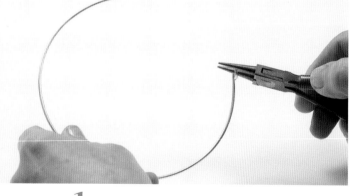

1 To make the tiara base, cut 12 in. (30 cm) of 12-gauge (2-mm) wire. Shape the wire into a curve by bending it around a jar or bottle. Using your round-nose pliers, form a link (see page 13) at each end.

2 Thread one of the 14-mm pearl beads onto the end of a spool of 20-gauge (0.8-mm) wire. Push the bead up the wire and make a small open spiral (see page 15) at the end. Flatten the spiral against the side of the bead,

3 Using your fingers, wrap the rest of the wire tightly around the perimeter of the bead until it reaches the opposite side.

4 Using your chain-nose pliers, bend the wire into a straight stem at 90° to the bead. Cut the wire from the spool, leaving about 2½ in. (6.5 cm) extending. Thread all the 14-mm and 8-mm beads in this way to make the pearl "buds"; you may find it easier to use thinner 24-gauge (0.6-mm) wire to thread the 8-mm beads.

5 To make the "leaves," work from a spool of 20-gauge (0.8-mm) wire and, using your round-nose pliers, make a small circle at the very end. Holding the circle in your flat-nose pliers, make an open spiral (see page 15) about ½ in. (1 cm) in diameter. Place the tips of your round-nose pliers about ½ in. (1 cm) from the spiral and bend the wire down and then directly back to make the point of the "leaves."

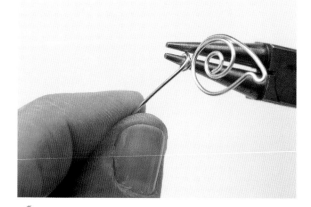

6 Bring the rest of the wire around the side of the spiral and form a small, complete circle at the base of the spiral, using the tips of your round-nose pliers. Straighten out the stem and cut from the spool, leaving about 2½ in. (6.5 cm) projecting. When you have made five wire "leaves," hammer the outer edges on a steel stake to flatten and work harden them (see page 15).

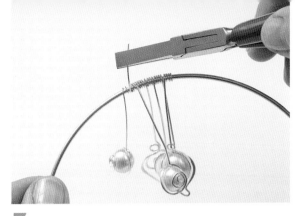

7 Starting in the center and working outward on each side, begin wiring the stems of the "buds" and "leaves" onto the tiara base, wrapping the ends of the wires around the tiara several times.

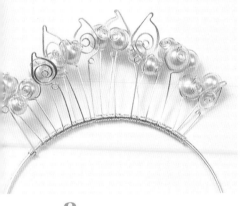

8 Stagger the height of the stems slightly, so that the tallest are in the center.

9 Cut about 20 in. (50 cm) of 2-mm round silver ribbon and attach it to one side of the tiara base with a sliver of double-sided tape. Wrap it around the tiara base, weaving it in and out between the beaded stems and decorations. Secure with more double-sided tape on the opposite side.

10 Cut 20 in. (50 cm) of 24-gauge (0.6-mm) wire. Wrap it around the ribbon, adding 6-mm pearls at intervals. As you get the tiara decorations, weave the wire in and out of the stems. This will help to secure them more firmly. Tweak and adjust the stems with your fingers until you are happy with the arrangement.

Leaf and flower necklace

This necklace is perfect for a plunge-neckline dress. The stylized flowers and leaves are bold, to match the Bud and leaf tiara on page 28, but you could simplify the design by making only one "flower" or the central pendent "leaf" and suspending it from a ready-made chain. Choose beads to match the color theme of your wedding and, to complete the set, add matching earrings.

You will need

20-gauge (0.8-mm) silver-plated
    wire
3 x 8-mm ivory pearl beads
1 x 5-mm ivory pearl bead
Ready-made silver chain
Wire cutters
Round-, flat-, and chain-nose
    pliers
Jig and 8 small pegs
Jig pattern on page 125
Hammer and steel stake
    (optional)

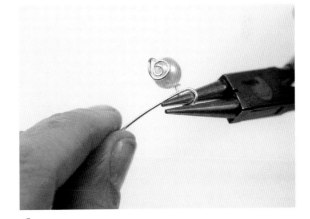

1 Following the pattern on page 125, place the pegs in the jig. Work out how much wire you need for each motif (see page 16) and cut a piece of 20-gauge (0.8-mm) wire to this length. Thread the wire with an 8-mm ivory pearl bead and make a spiral head pin at the end (see page 14), pushing it against the rounded surface of the bead. Using your round-nose pliers, form a link (see page 13) at the opposite side of the bead, so that the wire crosses over itself.

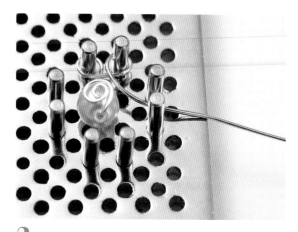

2 Place the loop you've just made over one of the pegs in the jig pattern, with the bead in the center of the pegs. Following the jig pattern, wrap the wire around the pegs. When you get to the very last peg, wrap the wire around it twice.

3 Remove the wire unit from the jig. Wrap the protruding end of the wire around the base of the first loop, cut off any excess, and neaten the ends. Stroke hammer the edges (see page 15) if you wish, but do not hammer any crossed-over wires or you will weaken them. Repeat steps 1–3 to make two more units.

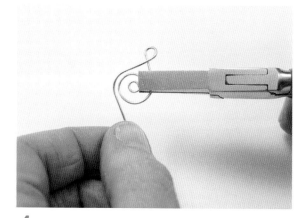

4 Working from a spool of 20-gauge (0.8-mm) wire, make an open spiral (see page 15) about ½ in. (1 cm) in diameter. Place your round-nose pliers on the spiral and bring the wire around until it crosses over itself to form a loop. Bring the working wire around the side of the spiral until it is opposite the loop, and cut from the spool. Using your round-nose pliers, form a link at the very end of the wire, curling back toward the spiral, so that it sits opposite the top loop.

5 Repeat steps 4 and 5 to create five more units; one unit is for the end of the clasp– this one needs to have a larger loop at one end. If you wish, stroke hammer the edges of the units to flatten and work harden, but don't hammer any crossed-over wires.

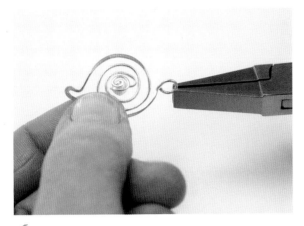

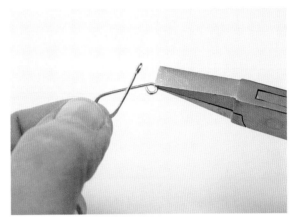

6 Using 20-gauge (0.8-mm) wire and a 5-mm ivory pearl bead, and following steps 1–3 of the Spring leaves card on page 26, make one "leaf." If you wish, gently stroke hammer the wire around the bead to work harden it.

7 To make a "hanger" for the central unit, cut 3 in. (7.5 cm) of 20-gauge (0.8-mm) wire. Place your round-nose pliers at the center of the wire and bring the wire around to form a loop. Use your round-nose pliers to make a link (see page 13) at each end.

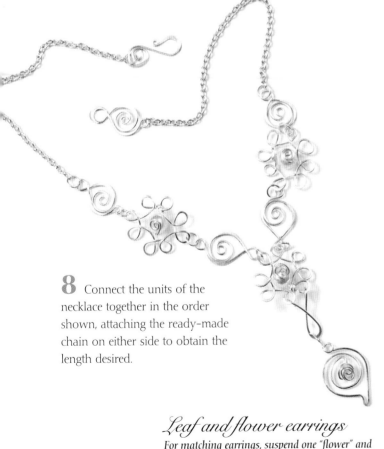

8 Connect the units of the necklace together in the order shown, attaching the ready-made chain on either side to obtain the length desired.

Leaf and flower earrings

For matching earrings, suspend one "flower" and one "leaf" from ear wires, attaching a pearl bead to the base of the ear wires if you wish.

Lily headband

This headddress looks stunning for flower girls but could also be made with faceted crystals for the bride–traditionally, the lily flower is associated with purity. Here, the pearly-white flower looks especially vibrant against the green crystal stamens within. This design also works for dressing up hair for a ball, prom, or any other special occasion, and feels much more secure than a hairpin.

You will need

26-gauge and 20-gauge (0.4-mm and 0.8-mm) silver-plated wire

Assorted cream pearl beads, 3–5-mm in diameter

Assorted 4-mm green crystal beads

Approx. 30 x 9/0 pearl seed beads

Ready-made metal hair band

Wire cutters

Round-, flat-, and chain-nose pliers

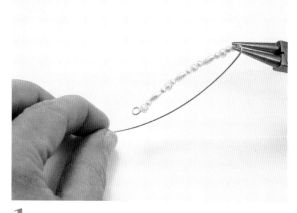

1 Cut 30 in. (75 cm) of 20-gauge (0.8-mm) wire. Using your round-nose pliers, make a small link at one end (see page 13). Begin threading the wire with cream pearl beads (I used 18–20). When you've threaded about 1½ in. (6.5 cm) of wire, bend the wire at 180˚.

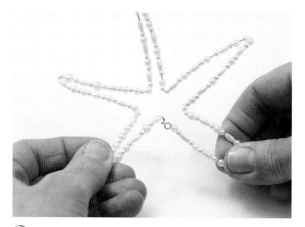

2 Thread on more beads to the same length as in step 1, then bend the wire back again in a zigzag fashion. Repeat to make five zigzags. Cut the wire and form a link at the end. Bring the ends together in a circle. Connect the links at each end of the wire together to secure the "flower" shape. Spend a little time shaping each petal with your fingers, opening up the centers and narrowing the ends into a point.

3 Cut 10 in. (25 cm) of 26-gauge (0.4-mm) wire and wrap the center of this wire several times around the center of the flower. Take the wire up the center of each petal, threading on more pearl beads as you go, then wrap it around the tip of each petal. Repeat to fill each petal, cutting more wire as necessary.

4 To make the stamens, cut 8 in. (20 cm) of 26-gauge (0.4-mm) wire. Bend it in half and push both ends through the center of the flower from the back. Thread pearl beads onto one end for about 1 in. (2.5 cm), then add a 4-mm green crystal bead. Fold the wire back around the green crystal, then wrap it around the stem in between the beads until you reach the center of the flower. Secure and neaten the ends (see page 14). Repeat with the other projecting wire.

5 Repeat step 4 to make a third stamen. Bring the unbeaded wire back through the center of the flower and use it to attach the flower to the side of the metal hair band. You may need to cut more wire to attach it really firmly.

6 Cut more 26-gauge (0.4-mm) wire and wrap it around the top of the hair band on each side of the "lily." Thread on beads, alternating pearl and green crystal beads. Make sure the beads sit on the top of the hair band, otherwise it will be uncomfortable to wear. If you run out of wire, cut another length and bind it over the previous one.

Birthstone bracelet

There is nothing more personal than creating
a special gift with symbolic significance. This
gemstone bracelet can be made using your
bridesmaid's birthstone and will
become a special keepsake,
in recognition of your
close friendship.

You will need

20-gauge (0.8-mm) silver-
plated wire

0.5-mm clear nylon
filament

Approx. 70–80 gem chips

9 x 4-mm pearls

6 x 1-mm crimp beads

Wire cutters

Round-, flat-, and chain-
nose pliers

Hammer and steel stake
(optional)

Pencil

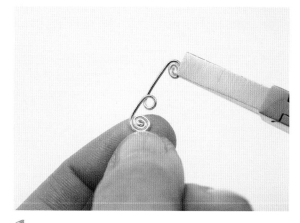

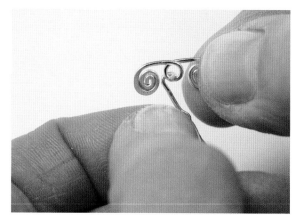

1 Begin by making a toggle clasp. Cut 2½ in. (6.5 cm)
of 20-gauge (0.8-mm) wire. Place your round-nose
pliers at the center and wrap the wire around to make
a loop, with the ends of the wire projecting straight
out on each side. Form a small, closed spiral (see
page 15) on each end of the projecting wire, curling
them in toward each other but leaving a small gap
between them and the center loop. Hammer the spiral
ends to work harden them if you wish (see page 15).

2 Cut ½ in. (1.5 cm) of 20-gauge (0.8-mm) wire.
Using your round-nose pliers, form a tiny link (see
page 13) on each side. Connect one of the links to the
center loop of the spiral unit that you made in step 1
to form the "T" of the toggle clasp.

3 Wrap the end of a spool of 20-gauge (0.8-mm) wire around a pencil and form a wrapped loop (see page 18) for the eye of the clasp. Hammer the end of the loop to flatten and work harden it if you wish (see page 15). Make two jump rings (see page 17). Attach one of them to the base of the clasp.

4 Cut three 9-in. (23-cm) lengths of 0.5-mm clear nylon filament. Thread each one through the jump ring remaining from step 3, feed on a crimp bead, then curl the filament into a loop and feed the end back through the crimp bead. Squeeze the crimp bead to secure. Thread each piece of filament with 3–4 gem chips.

5 Using 20-gauge (0.8-mm) wire, make six small coils in the same way as when making jump rings (see page 17). Thread one coil over all three nylon lengths, pushing it right up against the gem chips.

6 Thread each nylon filament in turn with a 4-mm pearl, followed by a second wire coil over all three lengths. Separate the filaments out once more and thread each one in turn with six gem chips. Repeat steps 5–6, pushing all the beads, chips, and coils up together, until you finish with three gem chips on separate filaments. Thread each filament through a jump ring and crimp bead, as in step 4, to secure.

Amethyst bracelet

Whatever stone you choose, the bold clusters of irregularly shaped gem chips are offset by the more delicate, rounded pearls and little silver coils. The amethysts used here are the birthstone for the month of February.

7 Attach the toggle clasp to the ends of the bracelet. If you wish, you can attach a hanging bead, charm, or a cascade of chips for extra decoration.

Pearly swirl bracelet

This eye-catching bracelet of pearls encased in swirls of silver is just the thing to draw everyone's attention down your arm to your ring! You can easily adapt the design for everyday wear by using colored beads.

You will need

26- and 20-gauge (0.4-mm and 0.8-mm) silver-plated wire

7 x 10-mm ivory pearl beads

14 x 9/0 clear seed beads

Wire cutters

Round-, flat-, and chain-nose pliers

Mandrel, approx. ½ in. (10 mm) in diameter

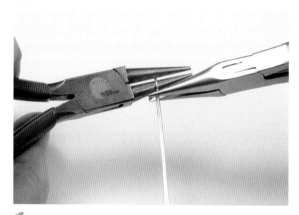

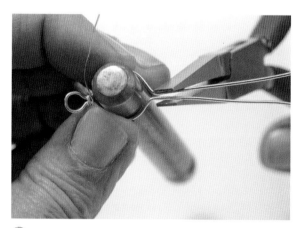

1 Cut seven 6-in. (15-cm) lengths of 20-gauge (0.8-mm) silver-plated wire. Place your round-nose pliers at the center of each length and, using the tips of your chain-nose pliers, squeeze the wires together around the pliers, to make a small loop.

2 Cut about 3 in. (7.5 cm) of 26-gauge (0.4-mm) wire and wrap one end around the base of the loop to secure; do not cut off the excess. Separate the thicker wires out in opposite directions and place the mandrel by the wrapped loop. Push the mandrel tightly against the loop and shape the wires around it. Using your flat- or chain-nose pliers, squeeze the extending wires together until they run parallel and straight.

3 Pull the thin wire (from step 2) down the center of the loop. Thread this fine wire with a 9/0 clear seed bead, then a 10-mm pearl, followed by another seed bead. Secure the wire at the base of the circle by wrapping it around the thicker straightened wires. Cut off any excess and neaten the ends (see page 14).

4 Form an open spiral (see page 15) on one of the projecting 20-gauge (0.8-mm) wires. Push the spiral over onto the surface of the 10-mm pearl bead.

5 Use your round-nose pliers to make a wrapped link (see page 18) with the remaining projecting wire. Repeat steps 1–5 to create seven "pods" in total, making the very last wrapped loop bigger than the rest, as this will be the "eye" of the clasp.

6 Make jump rings (see page 17) from 20-gauge (0.8-mm) wire and connect the seven "beadpods" together, attaching the unit with the largest end link at the very end. Make a toggle clasp (see steps 1–2 of the Birthstone bracelet on page 38) and attach it to the other end of the bracelet.

Bouquet brooch

I have been making "bouquet" brooches ever since I discovered wirework. As they have such a sense of occasion about them, I had to include this one as a design for the bride's mother's jacket lapel or hatpin. Alternatively, the beaded sprays can be wired onto the side of hair bands for flower girls' headdresses. You can make the spray as full as you wish.

You will need

- 26-gauge and 20-gauge (0.4-mm and 0.8-mm) silver-plated wire
- Approx. 12 x assorted beads, 8–10mm in diameter
- Stickpin finding
- Masking tape
- Wire cutters
- Round-, flat-, and chain-nose pliers
- Hammer and steel stake

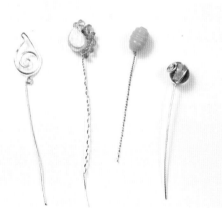

1 Make about 15 beaded stems in whatever combination you like. From left to right: a wire "spiral leaf" (see steps 1–4 of the invitation card on page 26, but omit the bead); a twisted stem threaded with tiny gem chips on one side; a single bead on a twisted stem; a single bead with a flattened spiral head pin. Small beads can be threaded onto 26-gauge (0.4-mm) wire, while larger beads will need 20-gauge (0.8-mm) wire. Leave a stem at least 2 in. (5 cm) long on each one.

2 Place all the stems and the stickpin finding together in a bunch and secure with masking tape. Working from a spool of 20-gauge (0.8-mm) wire, make a coil in the same way as when making jump rings (see page 17), large enough to slip over the stems. Cut the coil from the spool, leaving at least 2 in. (5 cm) projecting. Slip the coil over the stems and squeeze the top ring tightly with your chain-nose pliers to secure.

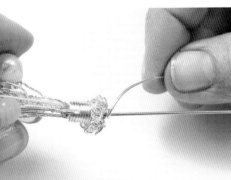

3 Make small, closed spirals (see page 15) with the stems projecting from the bottom of the coil and flatten them around the base of the coil.

4 Wrap the extending wire of the coil tightly around the stickpin finding. Cut off any excess and neaten the end (see page 14). Spend a little time arranging the stems, bending them and pulling them slightly apart to make more interesting shapes if you wish.

Table flowers

Whether you're hosting a small family gathering or a large wedding reception, you'll want to add a few decorative details to the tables to make the occasion extra memorable. These wire flowers look sensational pushed into low pots or vases with seasonal greenery —and, at the end of the day, your guests will be thrilled to take one home as a buttonhole!

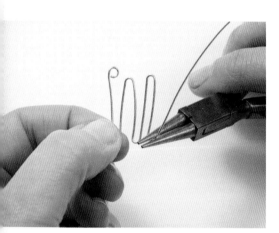

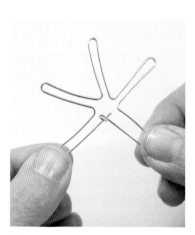

1 Working from a spool of 20-gauge (0.8-mm) wire, form a small link (see page 13) at the end of the wire. Place the ends of your round-nose pliers about 1 in. (2.5 cm) from the link and bend the wire. Continue in this way until you have made five zigzags. Cut the wire from the spool.

2 Using your fingers, pull the ends of the zigzags around to form a circle. Thread the cut end into the small link you made in step 1, then bend the cut end into a link to secure (see page 19). Spend a little time adjusting and shaping the unit.

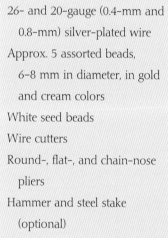

3 Place your chain-nose pliers in the center of each "petal" to open it up into a more rounded shape. Squeeze the very ends of each petal with your flat-nose pliers, leaving a small gap. Once you are happy with the overall flower shape, stroke hammer the petals on a steel stake to work harden them (see page 15) if you wish.

4 Cut about 10 in. (25 cm) of 26-gauge (0.4-mm) wire and thread this around the center of the flower to hold it in shape, weaving it in and out at the base of the petals. Leave any excess wire at the back of the flower.

5 To make the stamens, cut a 4-in. (10-cm) and a 6-in. (15-cm) length of 20-gauge (0.8-mm) wire. Fold the 4-in. (10-cm) length in half and push it through the center of the flower from the back, straightening the wires up through the middle. Curl each projecting end into a small circle as close to the center of the flower as possible, then thread on a gold-colored bead. Curve any remaining wire into a wavy tendril. The tendril will hold the bead in place.

6 Using your round-nose pliers, form a loop on the 6-in. (15-cm) length of wire 4 in. (10 cm) from one end. Push the shorter end of this wire through the base of the flower unit from the back. Thread the longer end with a bead and curl the rest into a coil or spiral tendril. Cut 10 in. (25 cm) of 26-gauge (0.4-mm) wire and thread it through the flower center. Weave the wire around the loop on the base of the flower, adding small seed beads as you go. Cut off any excess and neaten the ends (see page 14).

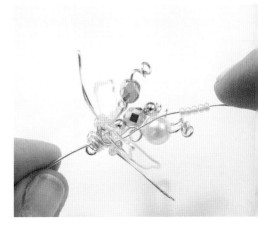

Chapter 2
SUMMER

Summer is probably the most popular time of year for couples to get married. The designs in this chapter include some vibrant summer colors—fuchsia pink, turquoise, lime green, zesty orange—as well as classic wedding-jewelry favorites, such as silver and pearl.

Butterfly card

Few things capture the spirit of summer more vividly than a brightly colored butterfly, so what better motif to include on a summer-wedding invitation card? I've used two vibrant, almost iridescent colors of wire–blue (for the groom) and pink (for the bride)–to create a pretty little butterfly with heart-shaped wings.

You will need

25-gauge (0.5-mm) pink and turquoise wire

1½-in. (4-cm) square of white backing card

3-in. (8-cm) square of patterned pink tissue paper

6 x 4-in. (148 x 105-mm/A6) card blank

Double-sided tape

Wire cutters

Round-, flat-, and chain-nose pliers

Scissors

Safety pin

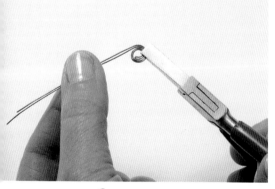

1 Cut two turquoise and two pink 7-in. (18-cm) lengths of 25-gauge (0.5-mm) wire. To make the heart-shaped wings, fold one turquoise wire in half and squeeze the ends together with your flat-nose pliers. Holding the doubled end firmly in your pliers, form a small, closed spiral (see page 15) about ½ in. (1 cm) in diameter.

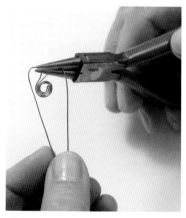

2 Place the widest part of your round-nose pliers next to the spiral and bring one of the wires around in one direction and the other in the opposite, until they meet to form the heart shape. Wrap one of the wires around the other a couple of times to secure, but leave 1 in. (2.5 cm) of each wire extending. Repeat steps 1 and 2 to make a second heart shape from one of the pink wires.

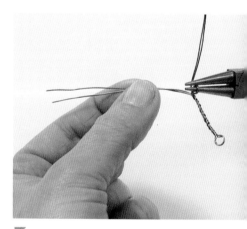

3 To make the butterfly's body, place the remaining pink and turquoise wires together. Find the center, then wrap the wires around your round-nose pliers to make a complete loop. Hold the loop and twist the wires together to make a stem about 1 in. (2.5 cm) long. Separate the wires out–one pink and one turquoise on each side. Place your round-nose pliers on each group of wires in turn and curl the wires around to create a complete loop, straightening the rest of the doubled wires to project above. These loops will be the butterfly's head.

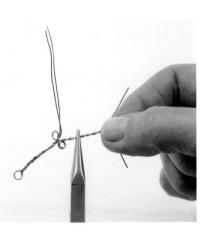

4 Hold the ends of each pair of wires in turn and twist to create the antennae. Curl a decorative spiral at the tip of each antenna.

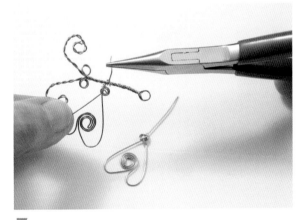

5 Spiral one protruding wire of each heart-shaped wing right up to the base of the heart, then wrap the other wire several times around the body of the butterfly to attach it. Cut off any excess wire and neaten the ends (see page 14).

6 Using a safety pin, make a hole in the square of backing card. Cut 1 in. (2.5 cm) of wire and bend it in half. Place the doubled wire around the butterfly's body, then insert it through the hole. Straighten out the wires on the back of the card, like the arms of a brad or split pin. Using double-sided tape, attach the butterfly on its backing card to a 3-in. (8-cm) square of patterned tissue paper, then attach the tissue paper to the card blank.

Eastern promise headband

For this design, I was inspired by the jewels worn on the forehead by ladies in India and, as these are typically associated with royalty and marriage ceremonies, it seemed appropriate as a bridal headdress. The sides of the chain are attached on each side of the head with hairpins. However, if you want to continue the beading around to the back of the head, just make the beaded chain longer. Alternatively, make this into a necklace design.

You will need

20-gauge (0.8-mm) silver-plated wire
10 x 4-mm, 2 x 6-mm, and 1 teardrop white pearl beads
Wire cutters
Round-, flat-, and chain-nose pliers
Jig and 4 small pegs
Hammer and steel stake

1 Following the pattern on page 125, position the small pegs in the jig. Work out how much wire you will need for each motif (see page 16) and cut a length of 20-gauge (0.8-mm) silver-plated wire to this length. Following the pattern, make ten "four-leaf clover" units, then gently stroke hammer the ends of each one to flatten and work harden them (see page 15).

2 Make jump rings from 20-gauge (0.8-mm) wire (see page 17). Use them to connect a group of five clover units together, then a group of four (see page 18). Attach the four-unit row to the five-unit row. Finally, attach the last unit to the center of the base of the four-unit row.

3 Thread 2 x 6-mm pearls and the teardrop pearl bead separately onto 20-gauge (0.8-mm) wire. Make a link at one end and a spiral-flattened head pin at the other (see page 14), then flatten the spiral against the front surface of each bead. Attach the teardrop to the central "clover" unit and the 6-mm pearl beads to the last unit on either side of the four-unit row.

4 Make eight spiral beaded S-links (see page 16), using 4 in. (10 cm) of 20-gauge (0.8-mm) wire and a 4-mm white pearl bead for each one. Connect them together in two groups of four, using two jump rings between each unit. Make a wrapped, beaded "eye" (see page 19) for one end of each group, and attach via jump rings.

5 Attach one chain to each end of the central unit, using two jump rings.

Sun-ray necklace

I designed this collar necklace to suit a strapless gown, a popular style for summer wedding dresses. The white pearls and silver beads that I've used look bold and will shimmer in the sunlight, but for something a little more subtle, use smaller beads and make the "rays" from pre-cut lengths of chain instead. This choker style epitomizes the Egyptian collar necklaces worn in ancient times; the bride can feel like a Sun Goddess at her wedding!

You will need

20-gauge (0.8-mm) silver-plated wire

0.5-mm clear nylon filament

9/0 white seed beads

6-mm silver beads

1 x 8-mm white Baroque pearl bead

Assorted white pearl beads

4 x 1-mm silver crimp beads

Wire cutters

Round-, flat-, and chain-nose pliers

1 Working from a spool of 20-gauge (0.8-mm) silver-plated wire, thread the end with a white seed bead followed by a 6-mm silver bead. Make a link at the seed bead end and a small spiral head pin at the other (see page 14) and turn the link so that it sits at 90° to the head pin. Make 14 units in this way. Then make a 15th unit comprising a seed bead, a 6-mm silver bead, and an 8-mm Baroque pearl bead, leaving a longer stem between the pearl bead and the link, as this unit will be the projecting center of the necklace.

2 Cut about 10 in. (25 cm) of nylon filament. Thread a crimp bead on at one end, then curl the filament into a loop and feed the end back through the crimp. Squeeze the crimp bead to secure. Thread seven of the linked beads onto the filament, followed by the longer stem unit and the remaining seven linked beads.

4 Thread a selection of pearl and silver beads onto 20-gauge (0.8-mm) wire, forming a link (see page 13) at each end of each unit. Connect the beaded units together to form a chain for each side of the necklace. (It is entirely up to you how long you choose to make the chains.)

3 Thread a crimp bead onto the end of the nylon filament, and then curl the filament into a loop and feed the end back through the crimp bead, next to the last bead unit. Squeeze the crimp bead to secure. Snip off any excess filament.

5 Connect the end links of the beaded chains to the nylon filament loops on each side of the necklace centerpiece. To complete the necklace, attach a fish-hook clasp and eye fastener to the ends of the beaded chain.

Matching set

Pearl and silver earrings complement the necklace beautifully, providing the perfect finishing touch to a design that is both elegant and timeless.

Flower power choker

Changing the color of the beads can completely transform the mood of a piece: made with white pearls secured on a silver stem with gold wire, the design looks stunning as a necklace for the bride (opposite). For young bridesmaids wearing colorful shades of pink or orange, the version to the right makes a dramatic style statement.

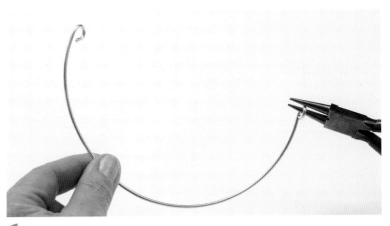

You will need

12- and 26-gauge (2-mm and 0.4-mm) silver-plated wire

25-gauge (0.5-mm) pink wire

Approx. 140 x 9/0 green seed beads

10–12 x 6-mm orange crystals

2–4 x 8-mm pink crystals

10 x 9/0 pearl seed beads

Heavy-duty and jewelry wire cutters

Round-, flat-, and chain-nose pliers

Color crazy choker
The punchy combination of pink and orange flowers and zingy green leaves makes this a perfect summery color choice.

1 The choker frame is made in two parts. Using heavy-duty wire cutters, cut a 10-in. (25-cm) and a 16-in. (40-cm) length of 12-gauge (2-mm) wire. Curve the wire around a large jar or mandrel to form a semi-circle. Using round-nose pliers, form a link (see page 13) at each end of the 10-in. (25-cm) length, making sure that the links sit at 90° to the wire and curve in opposite directions.

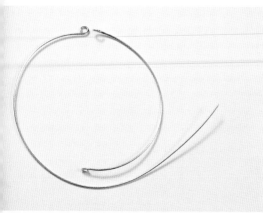

2 Make a link at one end of the 16-in. (40-cm) length; this link should not sit at 90° to the wire. Curve this wire so that it forms a mirror image to the first unit, as shown in the photo.

3 Using your round-nose pliers, create tapered "wiggles" with the projecting end of the longer wire, finishing with a small open spiral (see page 15).

4 Place the two wires together and spend a little time checking that they sit well together and will form a circular choker base when joined together.

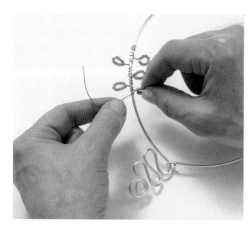

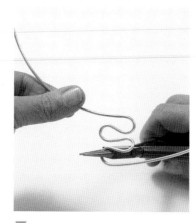

6 Repeat step 5 on the other side of the choker frame. Push the pink wires and beaded loops on both sides to the center of the necklace.

5 Cut a length of 25-gauge (0.5-mm) pink wire. Attach one end to one side of the choker base by wrapping it tightly over the frame. Thread the projecting pink wire with 11 green seed beads and bring the wire around to form a tight, beaded loop. Holding the loop with your fingers, twist it a couple of times to secure, and then wrap the pink wire around the frame again, bringing the projecting wire out on the opposite side. Repeat, alternating between wrapping the wire around the frame and making beaded loops, until you have made six "leaves" (cut more pink wire if necessary).

Bridal pearl earrings

Repeat the beaded flower motif and suspend from ready-made ear wires and a "leaf" unit to make matching earrings.

7 Now make two beaded flowers—one for the center and one for the side. Cut two 6-in. (15-cm) lengths of 26-gauge (0.4-mm) silver-plated wire. Thread each one with five 6-mm orange crystals and five pearl seed beads, alternating as you go. Bring the ends of the wires together, thread them back through the hole of the first 6-mm bead, and pull taut to form a circle.

8 Pull one of the extending wires into the center of the circle and thread it with an 8-mm pink crystal to form the center of the flower. Wrap the ends of the wire around the outer frame of the flower to secure.

9 Wrap the protruding wires around the choker frame, attaching one flower to the center next to the "wiggled" section and the second to the side of the choker.

10 For extra decoration, cut 8 in. (20 cm) of 25-gauge (0.5-mm) pink wire and use it to attach more crystal beads in the gaps between the wiggles at the front of the choker.

Pearl butterfly hairpin

You will need

26-gauge (0.4-mm) silver-plated wire

9 x 4-mm and 1 x 6-mm pearl beads

Approx. 150 x 9/0 pearl seed beads of your choice

Ready-made hairpin

Wire cutters

Round-, flat-, and chain-nose pliers

These decorative hairpins continue the butterfly theme of the invitation cards on page 50 and look fabulous pinned into an up-style hairdo. They can also be wired onto hairpins and bands and would look fantastic on longer stalks, pushed into floral bouquets or ribboned baskets as table decorations. You can, of course, make them in vibrant-colored bead combinations, to suit the color scheme of the wedding.

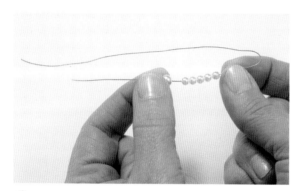

1 Cut about 10 in. (25 cm) of 26-gauge (0.4-mm) silver-plated wire. Bend the wire in half about 4 in. (10 cm) from one end. Thread the shorter end of the wire with five 4-mm pearls and one 6-mm pearl.

2 Wrap the longer wire around the shorter wire, in between each bead in turn, with a few more wraps just under the 6-mm pearl. Twist both wires together next to the hole of the 6-mm pearl, but do not snip off the excess wire.

3 To make the antennae, thread a 4-mm pearl onto each projecting wire and bend the wire around the bead to form a loop, securing it by wrapping it around the stem just above the 6-mm pearl.

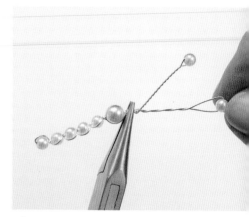

4 Hold one 4-mm pearl tightly with your fingers and twist, to create a twisted stem. Repeat for the second antenna. Neaten the ends of the wire (see page 14).

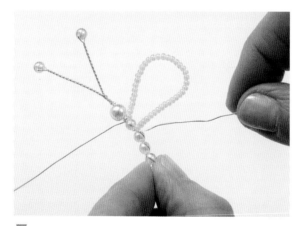

5 To make the top "wings," cut about 8 in. (20 cm) of 26-gauge (0.4-mm) wire and secure it by wrapping the center of the wire under the 6mm pearl, pulling the projecting wires out on each side. Thread each wire with about forty 9/0 seed beads to make a tightly beaded loop, and secure by wrapping the surplus wire around the stem, one bead down. Snip off the excess wire and neaten the ends (see page 14). Pull the wings into shape with your fingers.

6 To make the bottom wings, cut about 6 in. (15 cm) of 26-gauge (0.4-mm) wire and secure it under the 6-mm bead, as in the previous step. Thread each projecting wire with ten 9/0 seed beads and secure the wire around the bottom corner of the top wing.

Multicolored butterflies

For young bridesmaids, choose beads in colors that match the floral displays; here, the bright turquoise and pink seed beads would go perfectly with posies of scented sweet peas.

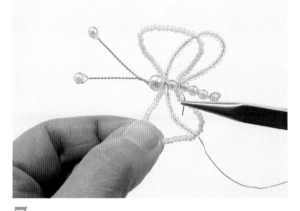

7 Thread another twenty 9/0 seed beads onto each projecting wire, then secure the wire around the base of the second bead down. If you have any wire left over, form it into a tiny spiral (see page 15) and flatten it against the butterfly's "body."

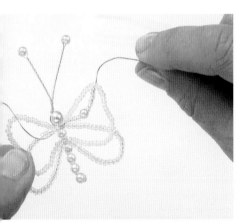

8 Cut about 5 in. (12.5 cm) of 26-gauge (0.4-mm) wire and secure the center under the first 4-mm bead. Onto each side of the projecting wire, thread four or five seed beads, a 4-mm pearl, then enough seed beads to fill, and secure at the tips of each top wing.

9 Cut about 5 in. (12.5 cm) of 26-gauge (0.4-mm) wire and wrap the center around the top of the ready-made hairpin. Twist the wires together to form one twisted stem. Wrap this twisted stem around the butterfly's body, just under the 6-mm "head" bead, to attach it to the top of the hairpin. If the unit feels a little wobbly, cut more wire and use it to bind another section of the butterfly's body to the hairpin.

Rose bracelet

This bracelet was designed as a special gift for the mother of the bride. Choose the central bead to match the color of her outfit and it will remain a treasured item long after the wedding. I've described it as a "rose" design, as the shape is reminiscent of stylized Art Deco roses.

You will need

20-gauge (0.8-mm) silver-plated wire

7 x 6-mm pink faceted crystal beads

Wire cutters

Round-, flat-, and chain-nose pliers

Hammer and steel stake

1 Working from a spool of 20-gauge (0.8-mm) silver-plated wire, thread a 6-mm bead onto the end of the wire. Using the widest part of your round-nose pliers, form a curve at the very end of the wire. Push the bead into this curve and then press the wire around the bead with your flat-nose pliers.

2 Holding the wire with your flat-nose pliers, spiral the wire around the bead (see page 15). Don't worry about keeping the spiral even–it can be a slightly irregular, random shape.

3 Wrap the wire around the shaft of your round-nose pliers to make a link (see page 13). Pull the wire around the side of the spiral and cut it from the spool, then form a second link, opposite the first.

4 Place the unit on a steel stake and very carefully hammer the outer wires to flatten and work harden them (see page 15). Keep your finger over the bead as you hammer to protect it from being smashed. You can be fairly random in this–leaving some sections unhammered will create an interesting contrast in texture. Repeat steps 1–4 to make five more units, making sure that the last unit has one larger link, as this will form the eye of the clasp.

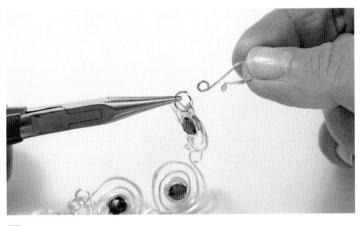

5 Repeat steps 1–4 to make a slightly smaller pendent drop for your bracelet, with a link at just one end. Make jump rings from 20-gauge (0.8-mm) wire (see page 17). Connect all the units together, using two jump rings between each unit and making sure the unit with the large link is at the end of the chain. Suspend the pendent drop from this link, then attach a fish-hook clasp to the other end of the bracelet (see page 18).

Twinkle-toe shoe clips

It can be hard to find a pair of shoes to match the splendor of a wedding outfit, but even a plain court shoe can be totally transformed with a clip studded with sparkling silver and pearl beads. An even simpler solution is to jazz up an old pair of diamanté clip-on earrings by adding extra wire, pearls, and crystals!

You will need

26- and 20-gauge (0.4-mm and 0.8-mm) silver-plated wire

Assorted silver and pearl beads (4-mm, 6-mm, and 8-mm)

2 x shoe clip findings (or large ear clip findings)

Wire cutters

Round-, flat-, and chain-nose pliers

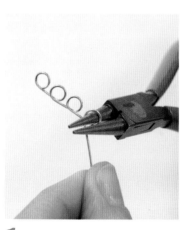

1 Working from a spool of 20-gauge (0.8-mm) silver-plated wire, use your round-nose pliers to curl a complete loop at the very end of the wire. Place your pliers just next to this circle and bring the wire around to form a second loop. Repeat until you have a row of ten loops, then cut the wire from the spool.

2 Bend the row of loops into a circle, overlapping the first and last loops, and join them together by binding with a 10-in. (25-cm) length of 26-gauge (0.4-mm) wire.

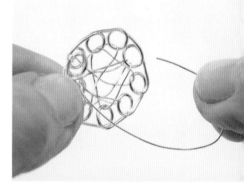

3 Weave the rest of the wire in and out of the loops, filling up the space at the center of the frame. This will create a mesh base on which the beads will sit.

4 Cut another 10-in. (25-cm) length of 26-gauge (0.4-mm) wire and attach it to the frame. Thread this wire with beads of your choice, looping the wire in and out of the mesh base and the loops around the edge to hold the beads in place.

5 When you have completely filled the center of the frame, cut more 26-gauge (0.4-mm) wire and use it to attach 4-mm pearl beads around the perimeter of the frame, wrapping the wire around the edge as you go.

6 Using 26-gauge (0.4-mm) wire, bind the shoe clip finding onto the back of the beaded circle. Repeat steps 1–6 to make a second shoe clip, matching the number and position of the beads as closely as possible.

Favor bag charm

Many people like to provide "favors" at a wedding—small gifts in a drawstring bag or box, to show appreciation for those who have helped with the organization of the wedding. This project is a simple but very effective way of enhancing a ready-made drawstring bag.

1 To make the lucky charm tassel, cut eight 1-in. (2.5-cm) lengths of chain and thread the top links onto the center of a 4-in. (10-cm) length of 26-gauge (0.4-mm) silver-plated wire. Cross the ends of the wire over each other to form a loop, then hold the lengths of chain in one hand and the wires in the other and twist the loop to form a twisted stem.

2 Cut 2 in. (5 cm) of 24-gauge (0.6-mm) wire. Holding the center with the tips of your round-nose pliers, curl the wire around to create a loop, then straighten out the projecting wires on either side.

You will need
(for each favor bag)

26-, 24-, and 20-gauge (0.4-mm, 0.6-mm, and 0.8-mm) silver-plated wire
9/0 pearl seed beads
2 x ¼-in. (5-mm) long clear bugle beads
2 x 2-mm, 1 x 6-mm, and 1 x 4-mm round pearl beads
1 x mother-of-pearl sequin
4 x 2½-in. (10 x 5-cm) drawstring favor bag
Ready-made chain
Wire cutters
Round-, flat-, and chain-nose pliers

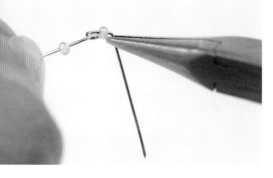

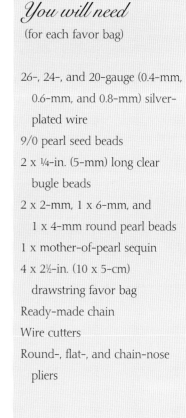

3 Thread a seed bead onto each projecting wire and push it up close to the loop. Using your chain-nose pliers, bend the rest of the wire below the seed beads at 90° to the loop.

4 Thread one bugle bead, two seed beads, and one 2-mm bead onto each projecting wire and form a small, closed spiral (see page 15) at each end to hold the beads in place. Bend the spirals outward to form the hands of the little figure.

5 Thread the central loop of this beaded unit onto the twisted wire stem projecting from the tassel, followed by a small seed bead, a 6-mm pearl bead for the figure's head, a sequin for the hat, and a 4-mm pearl bead.

6 Make a wrapped loop (see page 18) with the twisted wire stem at the top of the silver bead and neaten the end (see page 14). Make a jump ring from 20-gauge (0.8-mm) wire (see page 17) and attach it to the top loop of the lucky charm tassel, ready to secure onto one side of the drawstring cord of the bag.

Clip-on card holder

You will need

(for each clip)

20-gauge (0.8-mm) silver-plated
    wire
8-mm crystal bead
Wire cutters
Round-, flat-, and chain-nose
    pliers
Hammer and steel stake

This clip, into which you insert a slip of card bearing the guest's name, is designed to sit neatly on the side of a wine glass or champagne flute. Each guest can take his or her card holder home to use later as a bookmark or photo clip, as a memento of this special day.

1 Working from a spool of 20-gauge (0.8-mm) silver-plated wire, make an open spiral about 1 in. (2.5 cm) in diameter (see page 15). Place your round-nose pliers on the wire and bend the wire back around the spiral to form a U-shape.

2 Place your round-nose pliers at the top of the U-shape and bring the wire back around toward the base of the spiral.

3 Using your flat-nose pliers, bend the wire at right angles at the center of the base of the spiral. Cut from the spool, leaving about 6 in. (15 cm) projecting. Thread the projecting wire with an 8-mm crystal bead, push the bead right up to the spiral and, using your round-nose pliers, form a complete circle just under the bead to hold it in place.

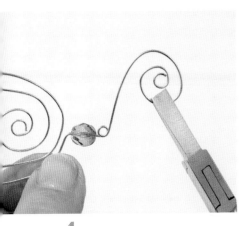

4 Make an open spiral at the other end of the wire, spiraling it right up to the bead.

5 Hammer both ends of the spiral unit to flatten and work harden it (see page 15), being carefully not to smash the bead.

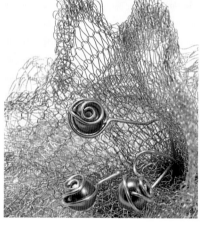

Chapter 3
FALL

Cheers!
Leafy crown
Chain link bracelet
Chain of hearts necklace
Leafy fascinator
Rosette corsage
Handbag charm
Heart napkin ring

With leaves changing color and glowing in the sunlight, Nature provides plenty of inspiration for weddings at this time of year. I've chosen ivory, gold, browns, and oranges—heartwarming combinations!

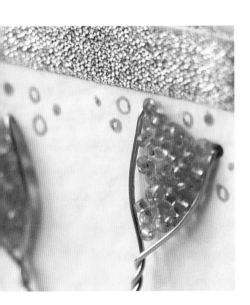

Cheers!

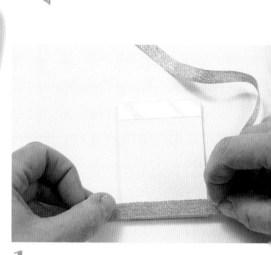

Get the wedding celebrations off to a fizzing start with this champagne-glass invitation card! The card design also looks very effective for birthdays and anniversaries and all special, celebratory occasions!

You will need

Gold ribbon, ⅜ in. (1 cm) wide

20- and 24-gauge (0.8-mm and 0.6-mm) gold-plated wire

11/0 gold-colored seed beads

2½ x 3-in. (6 x 7.5-cm) backing card

3 x 4-in. (7.5 x 10-cm) parchment-colored mulberry paper

6 x 4-in. (148 x 105-mm/A6) card blank

Wire cutters

Round-, flat-, and chain-nose pliers

Narrow double-sided tape

Scissors

Safety pin

Toothpick

White (PVA) glue

Gold gel pen

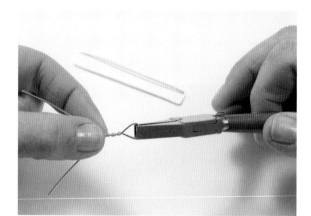

1 Cut two strips of narrow double-sided tape and stick one across the top and one across the bottom of your backing card. Peel off the backing paper and stick gold ribbon on top.

2 Cut two 5-in. (13-cm) lengths of 20-gauge (0.8-mm) gold-plated wire. Find the center of each. Using your flat-nose pliers, bend both wires up on each side about ¼ in. (5 mm) from the center, leaving a straight base about ½ in. (1.5 cm) across. Bring the projecting wires together, so that they meet leaving a triangular shape, and twist them together for about ¾ in. (2 cm).

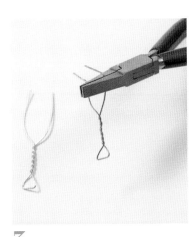

3 Use your fingers to curve the extending wires inward slightly, like champagne flutes. Using flat-nose pliers, bend the ends of the projecting wires at 90°, so that the sides of the flutes are about ½ in. (1.5 cm) tall.

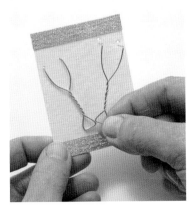

4 Using a safety pin, pierce holes in your backing card that correspond to the projecting wires on each flute and push them through. Bend and flatten the wires on the back of the card like the arms of a brad or split pin. Secure the wires on the back with double-sided tape.

5 Using a toothpick or the end of a piece of wire, apply white (PVA) glue to the center of the flutes. Sprinkle gold-colored seed beads on top and let dry. When dry, shake off any excess beads.

6 Tear a piece of parchment-colored mulberry paper to 3 x 4 in. (7.5 x 10 cm). Stick the champagne glasses decoration on top, using double-sided tape, then stick the mulberry paper to the front of the card blank. Draw "bubbles" coming from the champagne glasses using a gold gel pen.

Leafy crown

Every bride wants to feel like a princess on her special day, and this bronze and amber-colored crown, with its seasonal leaf motifs and delicate spiraled hearts, will do just that. The leaf design and color theme can be continued throughout the wedding accessories, including the table decorations and the bridesmaids' jewelry.

You will need

26-gauge (0.4-mm) gold-plated
   wire
20-gauge (0.8-mm) gold-plated
   and copper wire
Assorted bronze and amber
   faceted crystal beads, 4–8 mm
   in diameter
Heavy-duty and jewelry wire
   cutters
Round-, flat-, and chain-nose
   pliers
Hand drill and table vise
Hammer and steel stake

1 Cut four 12-in. (30-cm) lengths of 20-gauge (0.8-mm) wire–two copper and two gold-plated. Twist them together using a hand drill and table vise (see page 19). Separate the wires at one end of the twist. Wrap one wire around the twist two or three times, then cut off the excess and neaten the ends (see page 14). Repeat the wrapping process with a second wire.

2 Form a third wire into a closed spiral (see page 15), then flatten the spiral against the wrapped wires to hide them.

3 Make a wrapped loop (see page 18) from the fourth wire. Repeat steps 1–3 at the other end of the twist, making sure that the spiral and the wrapped loop are the same color at each end of the twist.

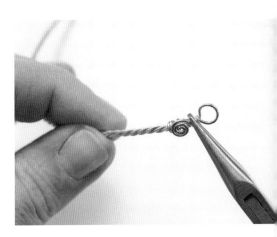

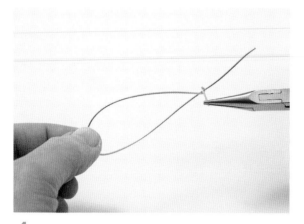

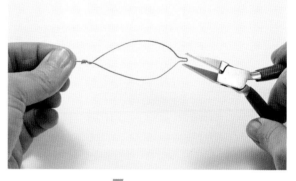

4 The amount of wire that you will need for the center decoration depends on how high you want the crown to be. I used 9 in. (23 cm) of 20-gauge (0.8-mm) gold-plated wire for the central leaf, two 7-in. (18-cm) lengths for the side leaves, and two 6-in. (15-cm) lengths for the smallest leaves. To make each leaf, fold the wire length in half to form a loop and wrap one end around the other to secure. Leave at least 1 in. (2.5 cm) extending from each loop to attach the leaf to the tiara base.

5 Squeeze the end of each loop with your flat-nose pliers, leaving a narrow gap at the tip. Use your fingers or pliers to open up the center of each leaf and spend a little time shaping them.

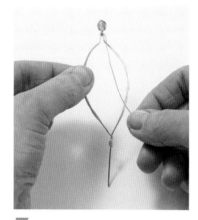

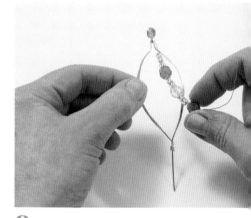

6 Hammer the leaves on a steel stake to flatten and work harden them (see page 15).

7 Cut enough 26-gauge (0.4-mm) gold-plated wire to stretch down the center of each leaf, plus about 2½ in. (6.5 cm) extra. Thread each length with a 6-mm crystal and make a tiny closed spiral head pin (see page 14). Place the crystal above the tip of each leaf and wrap the wire around the tip to hold the bead in place. Pull the rest of the wire down the center of the leaf.

8 Thread the projecting wire with beads of your choice until you reach the base of the leaf and secure by wrapping the wire around the frame. Cut off any excess and neaten the ends (see page 14).

9 Attach the leaves to the crown base by wrapping the stems around it, starting with the largest leaf at the center and working outward in descending order of size on either side. Space the leaves out so that the sides just overlap each other.

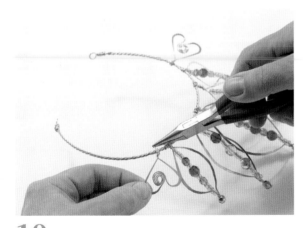

10 Cut two 7-in. (18-cm) lengths of 20-gauge (0.8-mm) gold-plated wire and make two identical heart shapes (see Chain of hearts necklace, page 82, steps 1–4). Attach the stems of these hearts to either side of the base, next to the smallest leaves.

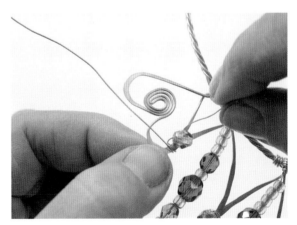

11 Cut six 4-in. (10-cm) lengths of 26-gauge (0.4-mm) gold-plated wire and bind the decorative leaves and hearts together, where the frames overlap each other. Add a crystal bead to each wire as you wrap, and use the leftover wire to wind around the perimeter of the bead to frame it.

Chain link bracelet

You will need

20-gauge (0.8-mm) gold- and
  silver-plated wire
7 x 4-mm clear crystals
Wire cutters
Round-, flat-, and chain-nose
  pliers
Hammer and steel stake

This stunning bracelet can be embellished
further by inserting drop pearls or colored
beads between the linked units. However,
if the bride is wearing a tiara and matching
jewelry, it's often best to keep the bracelet
simple and use wire throughout. Although
this looks complex, the "chainmail" effect
is created simply by connecting the
units together with pairs of jump
rings; the more jump rings you use,
the better it looks!

1 To make the beaded spiral S-links, cut six 4-in.
(10-cm) lengths of 20-gauge (0.8-mm) gold-plated wire.
Thread each length with a 4-mm crystal and then,
using the widest part of your round-nose pliers, form
a closed spiral (see page 16) on each end.

2 For the looped bar units, work from a spool of
20-gauge (0.8-mm) silver-plated wire. Using your
round-nosed pliers, curl a circle at the very end of the
wire, then place the pliers next to the circle you have
just made and bring the wire completely around the
shaft to form a second circle. Repeat to form a third
circle, then cut from the spool. Make 12 looped bar
units in total.

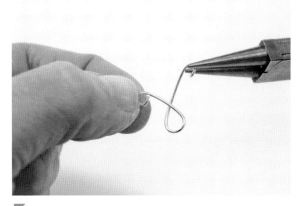

3 To make the eye of the fastener, cut about 4 in. (10 cm) of 20-gauge (0.8-mm) silver-plated wire and place your round-nosed pliers at the center. Bring the wire around the pliers to form a central loop. Using your round-nose pliers, form a link (see page 19) on each side of the central loop, curling the wire in toward the center. Stroke hammer the eye on a steel stake to flatten and work harden it (see page 15).

4 Make jump rings (see page 17) from 20-gauge (0.8mm) silver-plated wire–you will need at least 92! Using pairs of jump rings, connect all the units together as shown, alternating a beaded S-link and two back-to-back looped units. Make a fish-hook clasp (see page 18) and attach it to the other end of the bracelet.

Chain of hearts necklace

Designed to be worn with a curved neckline dress, this asymmetric necklace completes your wedding outfit with a hint of feminine dreaminess. Alternatively, you can simply suspend one of the heart motifs from a chain for a more classic and minimalist look.

You will need

26- and 20-gauge (0.4-mm and 0.8-mm) gold-plated wire

9/0 silver and gold seed beads

4-mm and 6-mm clear crystal beads

2 x 8-mm gold-colored faceted beads

Ready-made gold-colored chain

Wire cutters

Round-, flat-, and chain-nose pliers

Mandrel, ½ in. (1 cm) in diameter

Hammer and steel stake

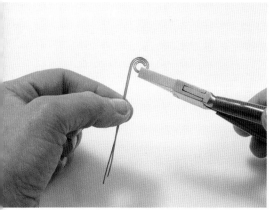

1 The front of the necklace consists of hearts in different sizes, all of which are made in the same way. Cut two 9-in. (23-cm), one 8-in. (20-cm), two 7-in. (18-cm), and two 6-in. (15-cm) lengths of 20-gauge (0.8-mm) gold-plated wire. Fold each length in half. Using your round-nose pliers, curl a circle at the end of the doubled wire. Holding it firmly in your flat-nose pliers, form a small, closed spiral (see page 15).

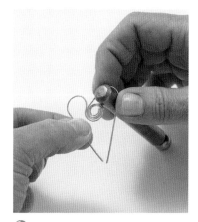

2 Place the mandrel next to one of the projecting wires and push the wire around it and down. Repeat on the other side.

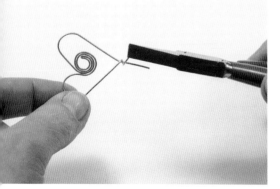

3 Bring the wires together to form the heart shape and wrap one wire around the other to secure. Neaten the end of the wrapping wire (see page 14), but leave the other wire protruding.

4 Hammer the outer frame of the heart shape on a steel stake to work harden it (see page 15). Form a link (see page 13) with the wire protruding at the base of the heart and twist it so that it sits at 90° to the heart.

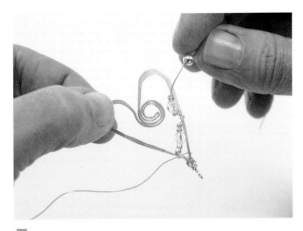

5 Cut about 9 in. (23 cm) of 26-gauge (0.4-mm) gold-plated wire and wrap the center of it around the base of the heart frame. Thread the wire with a few seed and crystal beads, then wrap the wire around another part of the frame to fix it in place. Continue, filling both ends of the wire, until you have as many beads in the center of the heart as you want. Cut off any excess wire and neaten the ends (see page 14).

6 Connect the hearts together in your chosen order by opening the link at the base of each heart, looping it over the side of the next heart in the chain, then closing the link again. I left one heart unbeaded at each end of the necklace and also included a couple of threaded beads to give an asymmetric look, but you can omit these if you prefer. Attach the ready-made chain to the sides. Make a fish-hook clasp and an eye (see pages 18 and 19) and attach.

Heart earrings

For matching earrings, an unbeaded heart shape, finished off with a tassel of ready-made chain, echoes the necklace motif without detracting from it.

Leafy fascinator

Fascinators are very stylish and contemporary-looking accessories, and this design–a smaller-scale and less ostentatious version of the Leafy crown on page 76–provides the perfect finishing touch for the bridesmaids' outfits. Why not make the beaded leaves on longer stems and add them to the bridesmaids' posies and bouquets for a matching finishing touch?

You will need

26- and 24-gauge (0.4-mm and 0.6-mm) gold-plated wire
9/0 peach-colored seed beads
Pale amber and bronze 8-mm crystals
Ready-made hair band
Wire cutters
Round-, flat-, and chain-nose pliers

1 Begin by making the leaf decorations. Cut one 6-in. (15-cm) and two 5-in. (13-cm) lengths of 24-gauge (0.6-mm) wire. Thread each length with 8-mm crystals and seed beads, alternating the beads as you go. Bend the beaded stem in half and bring the ends of the wire together to create a beaded loop. Secure by wrapping one wire around the other at the base of the loop. Leave the other wire extending by at least 1 in. (2.5 cm) to attach the leaf to the hair band.

2 Cut enough 26-gauge (0.4-mm) gold-plated wire to stretch down the center of each leaf, plus about 2½ in. (6 cm) extra. Thread each length with a 6-mm crystal and make a tiny closed spiral head pin (see page 14). Place the crystal above the tip of each leaf and wrap the wire around the tip to secure the bead in place. Pull the rest of the wire down the center of the leaf. Thread with beads, alternating one crystal and three seed beads, until you reach the base of the leaf. Secure by wrapping the wire around the frame. Cut off any excess and neaten the ends (see page 14).

3 Once you have completed all three beaded leaves, attach them to the side of the hair band by wrapping the stem wire around the band. Snip off any excess wire and neaten the ends (see page 14).

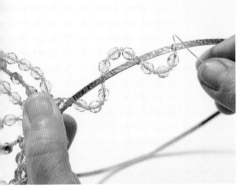

4 Cut 12 in. (30 cm) of 24-gauge (0.6-mm) wire and attach it to one side of the hair band, next to the leaf decoration. Thread the wire with three 8-mm crystals separated by a seed bead, to form a loop below the hair band, then wrap the wire around the hair band again. Repeat, threading on the same number of beads and forming another loop shape that sticks up above the hair band. Continue until you run out of wire, then repeat on the other side of the central decoration.

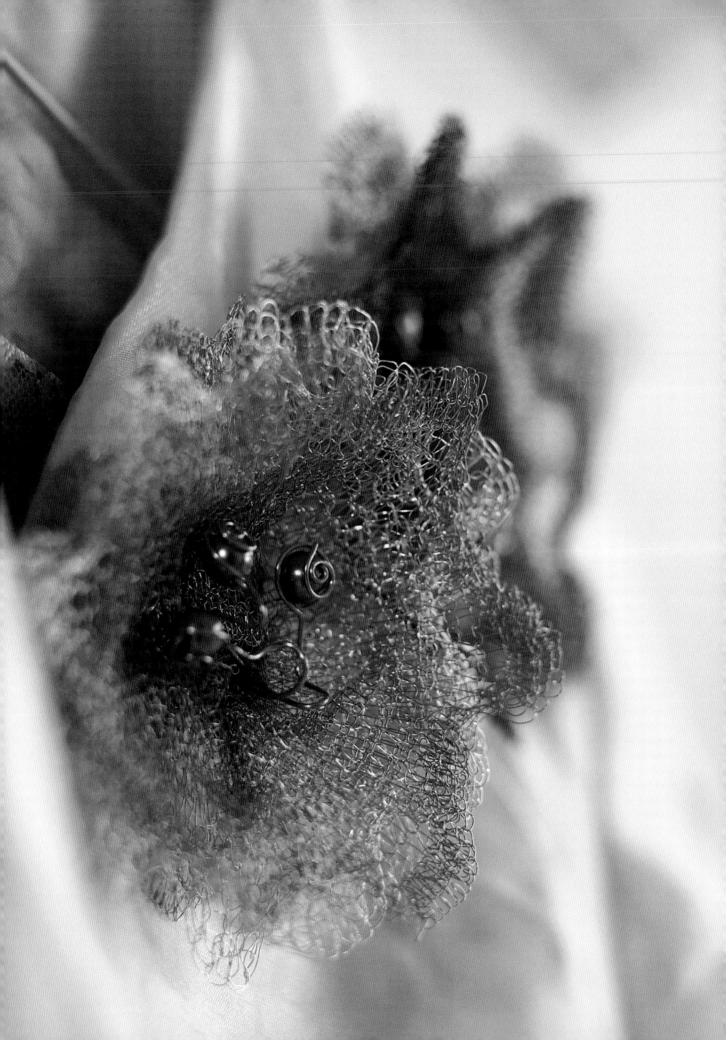

Rosette corsage

The bride's mother always wants to look her best on this most special of days, and this corsage, which can be pinned to a jacket lapel, dress, or hat, makes a dramatic and totally unique accessory. It is constructed from pre-knitted wire, which is readily available in tube form in every color of the rainbow.

You will need

Knitted wire in 2 blending tones
20-gauge (0.8-mm) copper wire
3 x 8-mm copper pearl beads
Ready-made brooch finding
Wire cutters
Round-, flat-, and chain-nose pliers
Scissors
Hammer and steel stake

1 Using a pair of scissors, cut a 7-in. (18-cm) length from each of the two colors of knitted wire. Using your fingers, fold one end of each one length over to form a double "hem."

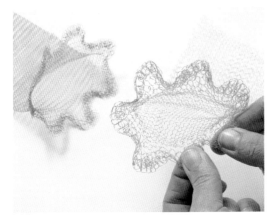

2 Using your fingers and thumbs, pull the edges of the "hemmed" ends out into petal shapes.

3 Gently stroke hammer the doubled-over petal ends on a steel stake to work harden them (see page 15). Do not hammer too hard, or you will break the wire.

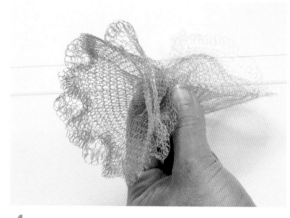

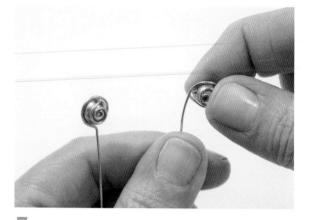

4 Place one tube inside the other and squeeze together to form a trumpetlike flower shape, such as a daffodil or lily.

5 To make the stamens, cut one 10-in. (25-cm) and one 5-in. (13-cm) length of 20-gauge (0.8-mm) copper wire. Bend the 10-in. (25-cm) length in half. Thread each end with an 8-mm copper pearl bead. Make a spiral head pin (see page 14) on each end, then flatten the spiral against the bead to hold it in place. Now straighten the doubled and single stems out with your fingers.

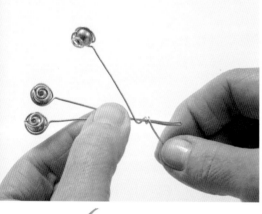

6 Place the stamens together and wrap the longer single stem around the end of the doubled 10-in. (25-cm) wire to secure in a bunch.

7 Place the stamens in the center of the tube of knitted wire. Squeeze the knitted wire around the stamens halfway down the tube to form the base of the flower. Cut 10 in. (25 cm) of 20-gauge (0.8-mm) wire and wrap the center of the wire around the base of the flower several times, making sure you wrap it around the stamens.

8 "Double-hem" the cut end of the tube of wire, as in step 1, then pull the layers out into petals, as in step 2. Fold the bottom half of the flower up over the top half, so that you have four layers of petals.

9 Cut 10 in. (25 cm) of 20-gauge (0.8-mm) wire and attach it to a brooch finding. Attach the finding to the back of the flower by weaving the wire in and out of the finding holes, through all the layers of the flower.

10 Using your round-nose pliers, bend the wire stamens into zigzag shapes. Adjust the overall shape of the petals with your fingers.

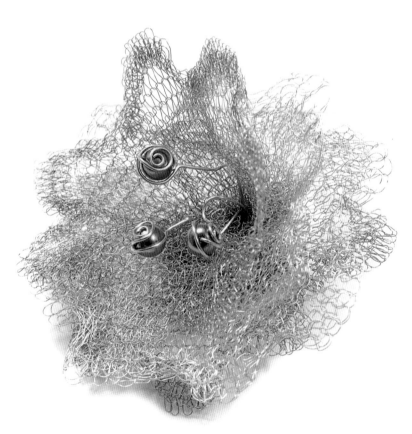

Handbag charm

A plain drawstring or clutch bag is a very useful addition to the bride's outfit, to hold a handkerchief, lipstick, extra hairpins, or a comb. A series of charms attached to a plain bag provides extra decoration and creates a personal touch. In this project I have combined heart shapes with rose quartz beads, as both symbolize love. Alternatively, why not follow the old rhyme and suspend four very different charms– "something old, something new, something borrowed, and something blue?"

You will need

26- and 20-gauge (0.4-mm and 0.8-mm) gold-plated wire
20-mm rose quartz stone bead
Rose quartz gem chips
Freshwater pearls
2 x 4-mm pearl beads
Ready-made gold-plated chain
Gold-colored clip or lobster clasp
Wire cutters
Round-, flat-, and chain-nose pliers
Hammer and steel stake

1 Cut a 5-in. (13-cm) length of 20-gauge (0.8-mm) gold-plated wire and thread on the large rose quartz bead, pushing the bead to the middle of the wire. Using your round-nose pliers, curl a loop in the wire right next to each side of the bead, securing it in place at the center of the wire. Make an open spiral (see page 15) with each of the projecting wires and flatten them onto opposite sides of the bead.

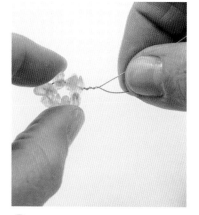

2 To make the rose quartz "flower," cut about 5 in. (13 cm) of 26-gauge (0.4-mm) wire and thread on 10–12 rose quartz chips. Bring the ends of the wire together and twist to form a circle.

3 Make a wrapped loop (see page 18) with the twisted stem and neaten the ends (see page 14).

4 Adapt or copy motifs from other projects in this section for the remaining charms. I made two hearts (as in the Chain of hearts necklace on page 82), adding a 4-mm pearl bead to the base of one stem and a rose quartz chip to the other; a pearl bead and a rose quartz chip on a twisted stem; and a pearl on a length of ready-made chain.

5 Make jump rings (see page 17) and connect all the components together in a cascade in whatever order you choose, with the clip or lobster clasp at the top.

Heart napkin ring

Made from intertwining strands of gold and silver wire, these heart-shaped napkin rings symbolize the bride and groom's love and commitment to each other. Quick and fun to make, they can be given to your family and friends as a keepsake after the reception.

You will need

20-gauge (0.8-mm) silver- and gold-plated wire

Wire cutters

Round- and flat-nose pliers

Hammer and steel stake

Mandrel, 1½ in. (4 cm) in diameter

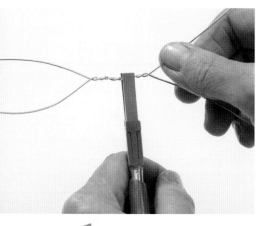

1 For each napkin ring, cut 8 in. (20 cm) each of 20-gauge (0.8-mm) silver- and gold-plated wire. Place the wires together, hold them in the center with your flat-nose pliers, and twist each pair of wires together in turn, stopping about 2 in. (5 cm) from each end. Make sure all protruding wires are the same length; cut them if necessary.

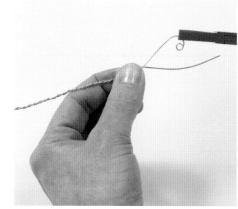

2 Using your round-nose pliers and curling the wire inward, make a loop at the end of each wire. Then hold the wire in your flat-nose pliers and begin curling the wire as if starting to make a spiral. When the two loops at the ends of the wire meet, the heart shape is complete.

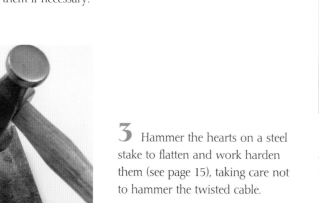

3 Hammer the hearts on a steel stake to flatten and work harden them (see page 15), taking care not to hammer the twisted cable.

4 Bend the twisted cable around a mandrel that is slightly smaller than you want the finished napkin ring to be, as the wire will spring open a little. The hearts should overlap in the center.

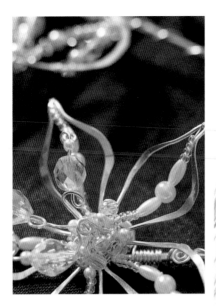

Chapter 4
WINTER

Frosted branch card
Topsy-turvy tiara
Winter garden comb
Winter sparkler necklace
Berry-bright bangle
Flower girl coronet
Icicle wand
Iced-leaf candle holder
Wedding cake topper

A winter wedding can be very glamorous and magical, with "ice" crystal jewelry and a faux fur wrap over a long white princess gown. I've added red to the white, crystal, and silver colors, to evoke the season's ornamental berries.

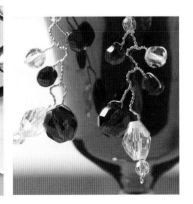

Frosted branch card

With its white-and-silver color scheme, this pearl leaf design is not only very appropriate for a winter wedding, but also looks wonderful as a Christmas card.

You will need
(for each card)

26-gauge (0.4-mm) silver-plated wire

2 x 6-mm white pearl beads

Approx. 96 x 9/0 pearly white seed beads

4½ x 2½-in. (11.5 x 6.5-cm) red backing card

6 x 4-in. (148 x 105-mm/A6) card blank

Masking tape

Double-sided tape

Ivory-colored organza ribbon, ½ in. (12 mm) wide

Wire cutters

Round-, flat-, and chain-nose pliers

Scissors

Safety pin

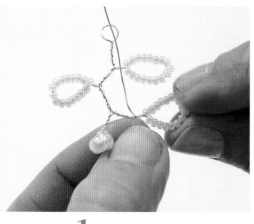

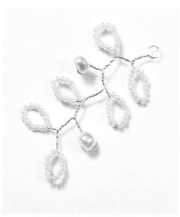

1 Cut 18 in. (45 cm) of 26-gauge (0.4-mm) silver-plated wire. Place your round-nose pliers at the center and bring the wires around them to form a loop, then twist the wires together for about ¼ in. (5-mm). Thread one wire with 16 pearly white seed beads, then bring the wire back around to the twisted stem to form a loop. Hold the loop in your fingers and twist it two or three times, then twist both wires together for about ¼ in. (5-mm). Repeat, making leaves on alternate wires.

2 Use 6-mm pearls instead of seed beads for two of the leaves. Cut a wavy line across the red backing card about one-quarter of the way up.

3 Thread a 6-mm pearl bead onto a 2-in. (5-cm) length of 26-gauge (0.4-mm) wire and make a beaded twist (see page 22). Then make a hole in the larger piece of red backing card with a safety pin. Push the beaded twist through the top loop of the frosted branch and then through the hole in the backing card. Bend the wire flat at the back of the card and secure with a sliver of masking tape. Thread a small piece of organza ribbon through the hanging loop of the branch and tie in a knot.

4 Attach the backing card to the card blank with double-sided tape. Stick the smaller piece of backing card below it, making sure it lines up squarely with the larger piece.

Topsy-turvy tiara

This tiara is dual purpose: it can also be turned upside down and worn as a choker necklace–hence its "topsy-turvy" name! If you feel it's necessary, you can add a safety chain and clasp to the back when wearing it as a necklace. In the demonstration below, I used clear faceted crystals to bring sparkle to a winter wedding.

Variation

For a more flamboyant version, use colored wire and opalescent pearls in toning colors. A matching bangle provides a finishing touch with a flourish.

You will need

26-, 20-, and 12-gauge (0.4-mm, 0.8-mm, and 2-mm) silver-plated wire

Assorted 6–8-mm crystal beads

Heavy-duty and jewelry wire cutters

Round-, flat-, and chain-nose pliers

1 Cut about 15 in. (38 cm) of 12-gauge (2-mm) silver-plated wire. (If you're not sure how much wire you'll need, use a piece of string as a measure.) Shape the wire into a curve by wrapping it around a cylindrical object such as a bottle or jar. Use your round-nose pliers to make a link (see page 13) at one end. Cut 11 in. (28 cm) of 12-gauge (2-mm) wire for the raised curve of the tiara. Shape this length into a curve, as before, and make a link at each end.

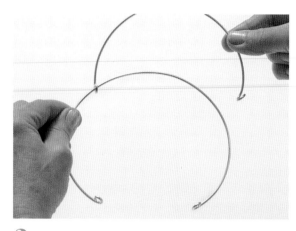

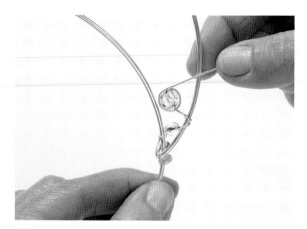

2 Thread the smaller curve onto the larger one and slide it to the center, so that the two lengths of wire make a crescent shape. Using your round-nose pliers, make a link on the cut end of the larger curve.

3 Keeping the smaller curve centered on the larger one, cut 20 in. (50 cm) of 20-gauge (0.8-mm) wire and attach it to one side of the crescent, leaving at least 1 in. (2.5 cm) of wire projecting. Bring the long end of wire into the center of the crescent, and thread on a crystal bead, wrapping the wire around the upper curve to fix it in place. Continue adding beads randomly, using your round-nose pliers to form circles on the working wire and wrapping the wire around the larger curve (the frame) as you go.

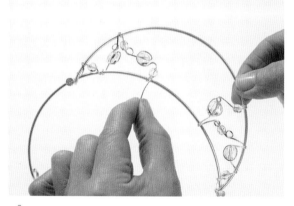

4 Repeat step 3 on the opposite side of the frame, again leaving a tail of wire at least 1 in. (2.5 cm) long. Make spirals (see page 15) with the short tails of wire on each side and flatten them against the frame to conceal any wrapped wires underneath.

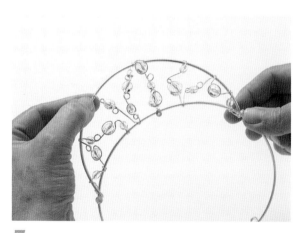

5 Continue threading, encircling beads and creating loops with your round-nosed pliers, until the crescent is as full as you want it to be; cut more lengths of wire if necessary.

6 Tweak the wire with your flat-nose pliers to create interesting wiggles and tighten the wire on the frame.

7 Cut about 20 in. (50 cm) of 26-gauge (0.4-mm) wire and attach it to one side of the tiara (next to a flattened spiral). Wrap the wire securely around the top curve, thread on a 4-mm bead, then secure the bead by wrapping the wire around the outer frame. Continue attaching beads all around the top curve, pushing them close together so that the curve is completely beaded.

Variation

Use the thicker wire to make a simple bangle frame and fill it with wire and beads in toning colors.

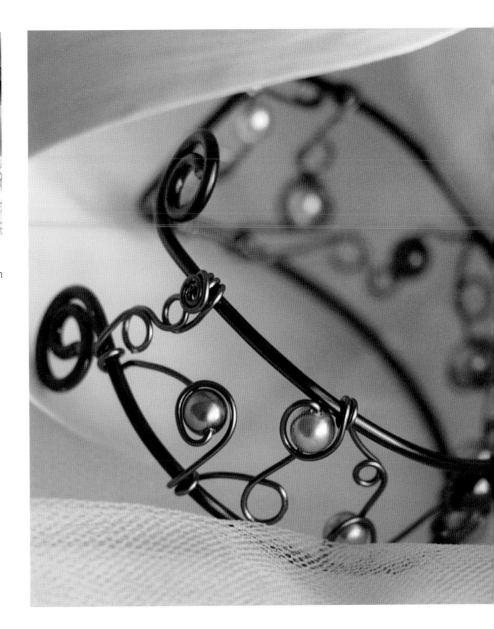

Winter garden comb

A comb is the perfect way to hold a veil in place and it's amazing how easy it is to design your own, to blend in with your color theme and style. Ready-made plastic and metal combs can be decorated with crystals and pearl beads, feathers, ribbons—anything you choose. To add a touch of "winter wonderland," I combined fabric flowers with my beads.

You will need

26-, 20-, and 12-gauge (0.4-mm, 0.8-mm, and 2-mm) silver-plated wire

Assorted 6–8-mm beads

Ready-made comb

Fabric flowers

Wire cutters

Round-, flat-, and chain-nose pliers

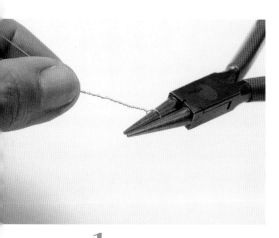

1 Cut five 12-in. (30-cm) lengths of 26-gauge (0.4-mm) silver-plated wire. Place the middle of each wire around one shaft of your round-nose pliers and twist both ends of each length in your fingers to create a twisted stem at least 1½ in. (4 cm) long.

2 Using clear faceted crystal beads, make each length into a beaded branch (see page 98).

3 Attach the branches to the top of the comb by wrapping the stem wires around tightly in between the prongs.

4 Attach fabric flowers in the same way, staggering the height of the stems (you may need to cut some of the flower stems down in size). Place the comb on your work surface. Where the beads sit close together, twist them around each other to hold the branches together more firmly.

Variation

Here, gold and holly-berry red beads make a dramatic color statement.

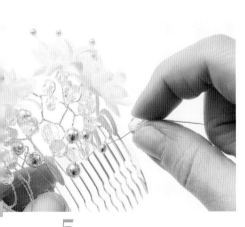

5 For extra decoration, cut a length of 26-gauge (0.4-mm) wire and attach a selection of crystal and silver beads to the top of the comb, making sure that they sit on the front of the comb.

Winter sparkler necklace

Like the invitation on page 98, this necklace features beaded "branches"–but these are made from faceted crystals, to add extra sparkle and radiance to the bridal accessories. Perfect for a V-necked dress, this design has a subtle, understated quality. You can use either clear, icelike crystals, as I did in the demonstration below, for that perfect wintery touch, or intersperse them with beads in winter-berry red, as shown opposite.

You will need

- 26-, 20- and 18-gauge (0.4-mm, 0.8-mm, and 1-mm) silver-plated wire
- 0.5-mm clear nylon filament
- 4 x 1-mm crimp beads
- Assorted crystal beads (4-mm, 6-mm, and 8-mm)
- Wire cutters
- Round-, flat-, and chain-nose pliers
- Hammer and steel stake
- Masking tape
- Superglue

1 Cut about 8 in. (20 cm) of 18-gauge (1-mm) silver-plated wire. Bend it around a circular object, such as a bottle or mug to gently curve it. This forms the base of the necklace.

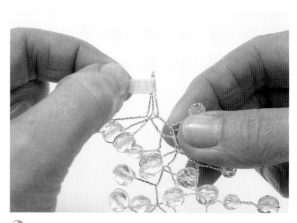

2 Cut two 18-in. (45-cm) and one 20-in. (50-cm) lengths of 26-gauge (0.4-mm) wire. Make three twisted beaded branches (see page 98), using 6-mm and 8-mm crystals in whatever order you choose. Place all three stems together, with the longest in the center, and tape together near the base of the stems with a sliver of masking tape.

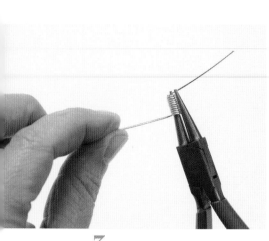

3 Using your round-nose pliers, make a coil of 20-gauge (0.8mm) wire big enough to fit over all the taped stems, as when making jump rings (see page 17), leaving a tail about 1 in. (2.5 cm) long at each end.

4 Make a small, closed spiral (see page 15) with one of the projecting ends of wire.

5 Flatten the spiral against the coil. Straighten the remaining protruding wire.

6 Push the taped stems in the coil and squeeze the top and bottom coils tightly with your flat-nose pliers to secure the branches inside. If you wish, you can dab a little Superglue inside the coil for extra security.

7 When the glue is dry, wrap the projecting wire of the coil around the center of the necklace base to suspend the twisted branches.

8 Spread the branches out on each side and wrap the nearest beaded stems of the side branches around the necklace base, leaving the longest stem projecting down the center.

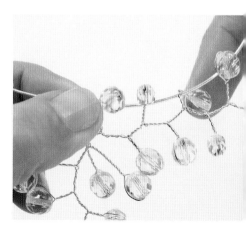

9 Alternating 4-mm and 6-mm beads, thread each side of the necklace base with extra crystal beads. Using your round-nose pliers, make a link (see page 13) at each end.

Variation
Single beaded branches attached to ready-made ear wires make really dramatic-looking earrings.

10 Cut two pieces of nylon filament (the length depends on how long you want the finished necklace to be). Thread each one with a silver crimp bead and feed it through the end link on the side of the necklace. Loop the filament over the link and back through the crimp bead. Using your flat-nose pliers, squeeze the crimp bead flat against the filament to secure onto each side of the necklace. Thread the filament with more crystal beads to obtain the necklace length desired.

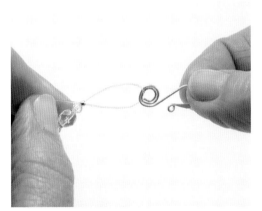

11 Make a fish-hook clasp and eye (see pages 18 and 19). Feed a crimp bead onto the end of the filament, thread on the clasp, feed the end of the nylon back through the hole in the crimp bead, and pull taut. Squeeze the crimp bead with your flat-nose pliers to secure. Attach the eye of the fastener to the other end of the necklace in the same way.

Berry-bright bangle

Twisting wires together to form thicker cables for tiara and choker bases, bangles, and rings is such a fun and instant thing to do. Topped off with ice-clear crystals and red beads as bright as a winter berry, this twisted bangle for the bridesmaids and flower girls is a simple, but striking, design that can be made in a matter of minutes.

You will need

20-gauge (0.8-mm) silver-plated and red wire

Selection of 6–8mm red and clear crystal beads

Heavy-duty and jewelry wire cutters

Round-, flat-, and chain-nose pliers

Masking tape

Hand drill and table vise

Mandrel

Hammer

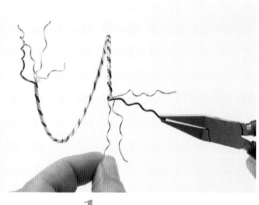

1 Cut four 12-in. (30-cm) lengths of 20-gauge (0.8-mm) wire–three silver-plated and one red–and twist them together with a hand drill (see page 19). Using heavy-duty wire cutters, snip off the taped ends. Wrap the twisted wire around a mandrel slightly smaller than the required bangle diameter. Using your flat-nose pliers, unravel about 1½ in. (4 cm) of wire at each end of the twist.

2 Wrap the protruding red wire around the stem, form it into a spiral (see page 15), and flatten it over the wrap.

3 Using your flat-nose pliers, straighten the other three wires as best you can and make a small loop on each wire as close as possible to the twisted cable. Thread a crystal bead onto each wire, make a spiral head pin to hold each bead in place (see page 14), and flatten the spiral onto the bead's surface. Repeat steps 2 and 3 at the other end of the bangle.

4 Wrap the bangle around the mandrel once more. When worn, the beaded ends will lock loosely together to form the bangle "clasp."

Flower girl coronet

Young nieces, sisters, and friends are always very honored to be asked to be flower girls, especially as it means wearing a beautiful dress. This coronet is designed to make a young child feel every inch the princess in a fairytale wedding. The height of the coronet can be altered and the design further embellished by adding more beads and crystals.

Variation

Bicone crystals—here in deep amethyst and luscious lilac—echo the shape of the triangular "peaks" and create a more angular-looking design.

You will need

26- and 20-gauge (0.4-mm and 0.8-mm) silver-plated wire

Assorted 4–8-mm crystal beads, including red beads

Wire cutters

Round-, flat-, and chain-nose pliers

Hand drill and table vise

Mandrel

1 Cut three 12-in. (30-cm) lengths of 20-gauge (0.8-mm) wire and twist together with a hand drill (see page 19). Bend the twisted wires around a mandrel to form the base of the coronet. Using your flat-nose pliers, unravel about 1½ in. (4 cm) of wire at each end of the twist and straighten them as best you can. Wrap one wire around the stems, cut off the excess, and neaten the end. Make a spiral on another wire and flatten it against the wrap.

2 Make a wrapped link (see page 18) with the last projecting wire on each side of the twisted cable.

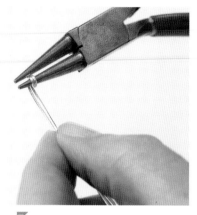

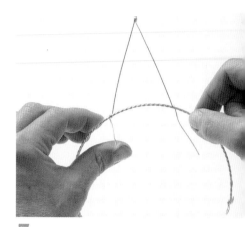

3 To make the coronet points, cut four 8-in. (20-cm) and one 10-in. (25-cm) lengths of 20-gauge (0.8-mm) wire. Bend each length in half and squeeze the wires together with your flat-nose pliers so that the wires run parallel. Place the tips of your round-nose pliers at the doubled end of the wires and form a link (see page 13).

4 Hold the link firmly in your flat-nose pliers and spread the wires on each side apart to make a triangular shape.

5 Decide how tall you want each peak to be, then attach by wrapping the ends of the wire around the twisted tiara base. Place with the tallest peak in the center. If you have any wire left over, form the ends into tiny closed spirals (see page 15) and flatten them against the tiara base.

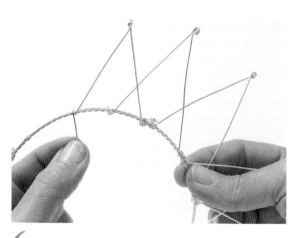

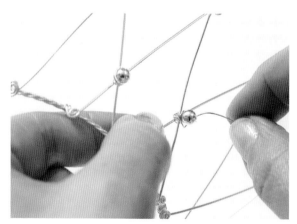

6 Attach the remaining peaks to the base in the same way, overlapping each one over its neighbor.

7 Cut four 3½-in. (9-cm) lengths of 26-gauge (0.4-mm) wire. Where the peaks overlap, wrap the center of the wire around both sides just once, to secure and to hold the peaks together. Then use one end of the wire to bind the peaks together really firmly and thread the other wire with a 6-mm bead, wrapping the rest of the wire tightly around the perimeter of each bead to make a "nest" or frame around it.

Variation

Here, the sides of the peaks are beaded with clear bugle beads, the effect being that the colored crystals almost appear to be floating in thin air.

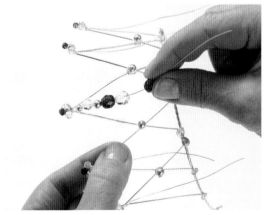

8 Cut five 5-in. (13-cm) lengths of 26-gauge (0.4-mm) wire. Wrap each one around the base of each doubled top link about 1½ in. (4 cm) from the end of the wire. Thread a 4-mm clear, a 4-mm red, and another 4-mm clear crystal onto the shorter end of the wire, then thread the wire back through the doubled link and wrap it around the base again to secure.

9 Pull the rest of the thin wire down the center of each peak and thread with beads of your choice, keeping the arrangement symmetrical so that peaks 1 and 5 are the same, and peaks 2 and 4 are the same. For impact, include more red beads in the tallest, central peak.

Icicle wand

Although fresh flower posies and baskets are more traditional for young flower girls and bridesmaids, if the child is very young, a wand is a fun accessory and can be kept as a "dressing-up" item after the special event. I chose a stylized ice crystal design to blend with the overall winter theme, but you could use a butterfly or flower motif (opposite) as an alternative.

You will need

- 26-, 20-, and 12-gauge (0.4-mm, 0.8-mm, and 2-mm) silver-plated wire
- 12 x 6-mm and 1 x 8-mm red bicone crystal beads
- 12 x 4-mm silver beads
- 6 x clear bugle beads
- Approx. 100 x 9/0 clear seed beads
- 8 x 4-mm clear crystal beads
- Red organza ribbon
- Heavy-duty and jewelry wire cutters
- Round-, flat-, and chain-nose pliers

Variations

Adapt other designs, such as the pearl butterfly hairpin on page 60 or a beaded flower, to use as the centerpiece of your wand. Just remember to keep the motif in proportion with the rest of the wand, so that it is not too top-heavy.

1 Cut three 3-in. (8-cm) lengths of 20-gauge (0.8-mm) silver-plated wire. Overlap them as shown to form a six-pointed "star" shape and bind together, using about 5 in. (13 cm) of 26-gauge (0.4-mm) wire and weaving the fine wire between the radiating wires to secure.

2 Thread each projecting length of 20-gauge (0.8-mm) wire with a 6-mm bicone crystal, a 4-mm silver bead, a clear bugle bead, another 4-mm silver bead, and finally another crystal. Make a head pin (see page 14) at the end of each wire and carefully flatten it against the top bead.

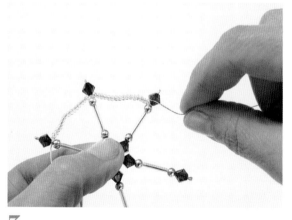

3 Cut about 10 in. (25 cm) of 26-gauge (0.4-mm) wire. Wrap the center of the wire around one of the top bicone crystals. Thread with clear seed beads, then wrap the wire about the tip of the next bicone crystal. Repeat until you have beaded the whole of the outer frame. Push the beaded wires in slightly with your fingertips to form a curve.

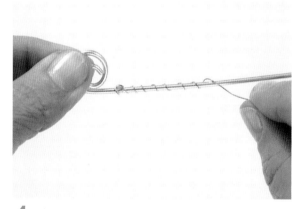

4 To make the wand handle, using heavy-duty wire cutters, cut about 12 in. (30 cm) of 12-gauge (2-mm) wire. Using your round-nose pliers, form an open spiral (see page 15) at one end, using about 2 in. (5 cm) of the wire, and make a link (see page 13) at the other. Cut about 18 in. (45 cm) of 26-gauge (0.4-mm) wire and start wrapping it around the spiral end of the wand, leaving even spaces as you go. If you run out of wire, just cut more and continue. Secure the wire around the top link of the wand.

Variations

Although these designs may look elaborate, the basic technique of wiring the motif to the shaft of the wand is very easy to master; just make sure that you neaten and secure any loose ends of wire firmly so that they cannot snag on clothing or scratch the young wand bearer. Bold, simple shapes make the best motifs:

flowers and butterflies are always popular, but hearts or stars would also work well. As with all the designs in this book, you can change the look completely by using colored wire and beads, so your fairytale princess can have a wand to suit every dressing-up outfit she possesses!

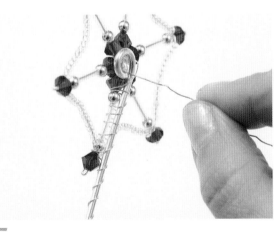

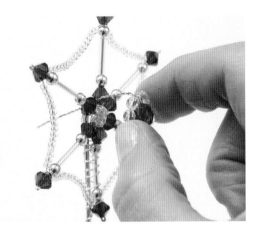

5 Place the center of the beaded icicle over the top link of the wand and one of the radiating stalks over the wand stem. Wrap 26-gauge (0.4-mm) wire around both the stalk and stem to secure together, taking the wire back and forth through the top link as if "sewing" it on. Cut off any excess wire and neaten the end (see page 14).

6 Using a red 8-mm crystal and clear 4-mm crystals, make a beaded flower with a twisted stem (see page 22). Push the stem into the center of the ice crystal, and push the flower down to hide the wraps underneath. Bring the wire stem back to the front again and wrap it around under the center of the flower to secure it in place. Tie a red organza ribbon around the stem, just under the ice crystal, to complete.

Iced-leaf candle holder

When you are hosting a wedding reception, extra decorative details on each table add an instant "wow" factor. These little tealight candle holders are perfect table garnishes. This design is extremely adaptable: you can substitute any motif–flowers, butterflies, fall leaves–for the frosted branches shown here.

You will need

26- and 20-gauge (0.4-mm and 0.8-mm) silver-plated wire

Assorted 4–8-mm clear crystal beads

Pearl seed beads

Tealight candle

Wire cutters

Round-, flat-, and chain-nose pliers

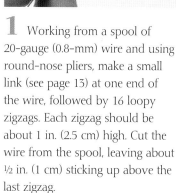

1 Working from a spool of 20-gauge (0.8-mm) wire and using round-nose pliers, make a small link (see page 13) at one end of the wire, followed by 16 loopy zigzags. Each zigzag should be about 1 in. (2.5 cm) high. Cut the wire from the spool, leaving about ½ in. (1 cm) sticking up above the last zigzag.

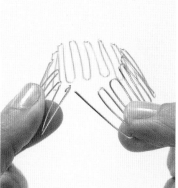

2 Join the ends of the wire together to make a circular shape. Stretch the loops until they fit snugly around the tealight.

3 Cut five 12-in. (30-cm) lengths of 26-gauge (0.4-mm) wire and make them into twisted "branches" with beaded leaves (see page 98), placing a small crystal bead at the top of each branch and using pearl seed beads for the leaves. Attach the branches to the sides of the frame by wrapping the stem around it several times.

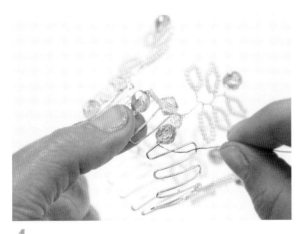

4 Cut about 12 in. (30 cm) of 26-gauge (0.4-mm) wire and begin weaving it in and out of the zigzag frame to make it more rigid and secure, threading on beads at intervals for extra decoration.

Wedding cake topper

Although these pearl and crystal hearts are the ultimate wedding cake topper, many of the other projects in this book can be

adapted to suit the same design: the Bouquet brooch (page 44), the Pearl butterfly hairpin (page 60), or the leaf motifs of the Leafy crown (page 76) and the Leafy fascinator (page 86). You can customize the design by adding feathers, flowers, natural green foliage, or ribbon to the base of the decoration.

You will need

26-, 20-, and 14-gauge (0.4-mm, 0.8-mm, and 1.5-mm) silver-plated wire

Assorted pearl, crystal, and silver beads

3 feathers

Heavy-duty and jewelry wire cutters

Round-, flat-, and chain-nose pliers

Hammer and steel stake

Masking tape

Large felt-tip pen

1 Cut two 12-in. (30-cm) and five 10-in. (25-cm) lengths of 14-gauge (1.5-mm) wire. Make a large, open spiral (see page 15) about 1 in. (2.5 cm) in diameter at one end of each of the 10-in. (25-cm) lengths. Hammer the spirals on a steel stake to work harden and flatten them (see page 15).

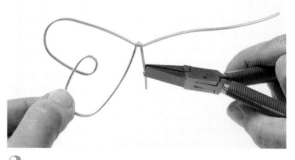

2 Make heart shapes out of the 12-in. (30-cm) lengths, making one heart slightly larger than the other and leaving a 4-in. (10-cm) stem projecting from each one. Hammer the heart shapes if you wish.

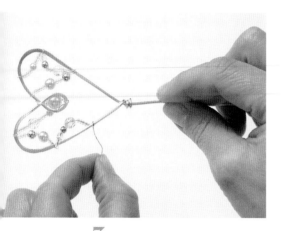

3 Cut a 10-in. (25-cm) length of 26-gauge (0.4-mm) wire and attach it to the side of one of the heart frames. Thread the wire with assorted beads, binding and attaching to the sides of the frame as you fill the center of the frame. Include a large ivory pearl at the center of the heart. Cut more wire if necessary–it's entirely up to you how many beads you put on. Repeat to fill the second heart shape with beads.

4 Place all the stems of the hearts and spirals in a bunch and tape together. Cut about 8 in. (20 cm) of 20-gauge (0.8-mm) wire and wrap it over the taped area.

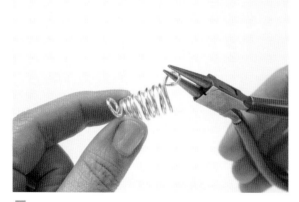

5 Working from a spool of 14-gauge (1.5-mm) wire, wrap the wire 8–10 times around a large felt-tip pen to make a coil, leaving a 1-in. (2.5-cm) tail at each end. Using your round-nose pliers, curl each cut end into a link (see page 13) and bend one of the links at 90° to the coil.

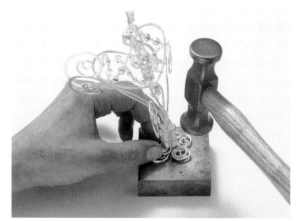

6 Push all the stems into the coil. Form the end of each stem into an open spiral (see page 15). Bend each spiral at 90° to the stem, and hammer the ends to flatten and work harden them (see page 15). These spirals will form the base of the decoration, so adjust them as necessary until it stands steady. For a final flourish, push three feathers into the coil stand.

Jig patterns

The patterns shown here are based on a jig in which the holes are arranged in horizontal rows. If your jig has holes arranged on the diagonal, simply rotate it until the holes are aligned as shown.

Curl the wire around the pegs as shown, following the direction of the arrows.

Eastern promise headband
(page 52)

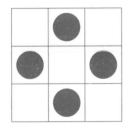

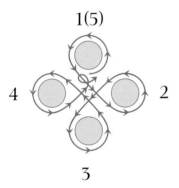

Leaf and flower necklace
(page 32)

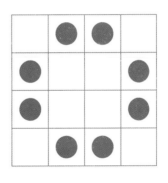

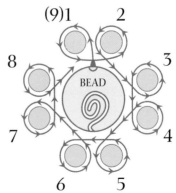

Useful addresses

Wirejewellery.co.uk
Tel: 01732 850 727
www.wirejewellery.co.uk
Tiara & wedding jewelry workshops.

The WireWorkers Guild
www.wireworkersguild.blogspot.com

US SUPPLIERS

Fire Mountain Gems
1 Fire Mountain Way
Grants Pass, OR 97526–2373
Tel: 800-355-2137
www.firemountaingems.com

Jewelry Supply
Roseville, CA 95678
Tel: 916-780-9610
www.jewelrysupply.com

Michaels
www.michaels.com
Visit the website for store
locations nationwide.

Mode Beads
5111–4th Avenue
Brooklyn, NY 11220
Tel: 718-765-0124
www.modebeads.com

Rings & Things
PO Box 450
Spokane, WA 99210–0450
Tel: 800-366-2156
www.rings-things.com

Rio Grande
7500 Bluewater Road, NW
Albuquerque, NM 87121
Tel: 800-545-6566
www.riogrande.com

Thunderbird Supply Company
Main tel: 800-545-7968

(Gallup location)
1907 W. Historic Route 66
Gallup, NM 87301
Tel: 505-722-4323

(Albuquerque location)
2311 Vassar NE
Albuquerque, NM 87107
Tel: 505-884-7770

(Flagstaff location)
2227 E. 7th Avenue
Flagstaff, AZ 86004
Tel: 928-526-2439
www.thunderbirdsupply.com

Wig Jig
24165 IH-10 West, Suite 217-725
San Antonio, TX 78257-1160
Tel: 800-579-9473
www.wigjig.com

UK SUPPLIERS

Beads Direct
10 Duke Street
Loughborough
Leicestershire LE11 1ED
Tel: 01509 218028
www.beadsdirect.co.uk

Cookson Precious Metals
59-83 Vittoria Street
Birmingham B1 3NZ
Tel: 0845 100 1122
www.cooksongold.com
Supplier of jewelry tools
and precious wires.

Creative Beadcraft Ltd
Unit 2, Asheridge Business Centre
Asheridge Road
Chesham
Buckinghamshire HP5 2PT
Tel: 01494 778818

(London location)
1 Marshall Street
London W1F 9BA
Tel: 0207 734 1982
www.creativebeadcraft.co.uk

Jilly Beads Ltd
1 Anstable Road
Morecambe
Lancashire LA4 6TG
Tel: 01524 412728
www.jillybeads.co.uk

Mad Cow Beads
The Bull Pen
Great Larkhill Farm
Long Newnton, Tetbury
Gloucestershire GL8 8SY
Tel: 0844 357 0943
www.madcowbeads.com

Scientific Wire Company
Unit 3 Zone A
Chelmsford Road Industrial Estate
Great Dunmow
Essex CM6 1HD
Tel: 01371 238013
www.wires.co.uk
Suppliers of knitted craft wire,
plus all types of wires.

TiaraMaking.com
Merchant House
1 John Street
Bamber Bridge, Preston
Lancashire PR5 6TJ
Tel: 01772 620772
www.tiaramaking.com

Index

Acknowledgments

Thanks to everyone at CICO Books who helped
with this edition, particularly Carmel Edmonds,
and not to mention Cindy Richards for allowing
me the freedom and opportunity to share my
designs. Also, a very special thanks goes to Sarah
Hoggett for her superb editing, and to Geoff Dann
and Stuart West for their sublime photography.